CORPUS CHRISTI

MAGDALENE

KING'S

QUEENS'

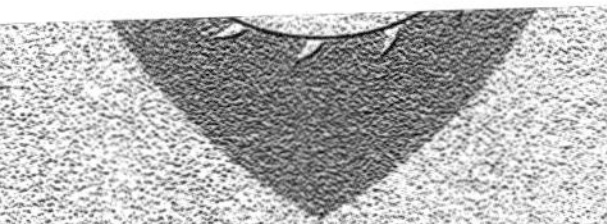
ST CATHARINE'S

DOWNING

GIRTON

NEWNHAM

SELWYN

HUGHES HALL

WOLFSON

LUCY CAVENDISH

FITZWILLIAM

HOMERTON

ROBINSON

CAMBRIDGE

in a new light

Photography by Andrew Pearce

Fotogenix Publishing

This book is dedicated
to all those who work to preserve the beauty of Cambridge

The 'Mathematical' Bridge, Queens' College

Text first published as *Cambridge: A Photographic Portrait* in Great Britain 2015,
Reprinted in 2018 as *Cambridge in a New Light*, with all new images
01767 677086
www.fotogenix.co.uk

Author: Debi Pearce
Editing: Sheila Bounford
Fonts: Cormorant, Cinzel, Jellyka BeesAntique handwriting
Printed by Swallowtail, Norfolk

ISBN 978-0-9547355-6-2

Photographs reproduced by kind permission of the Masters, Principals, Presidents, Provosts, Fellows and Scholars of Peterhouse, Clare College, Pembroke College, Gonville & Caius College, Trinity Hall, Corpus Christi, Magdalene College, King's College, Queens' College, St Catharine's College, Jesus College, Christ's College, St John's College, Trinity College, Emmanuel College, Sidney Sussex College, Downing College, Newnham College, Selwyn College, Hughes Hall, St Edmund's College, Murray Edwards College, Churchill College, Darwin College, Lucy Cavendish College, Wolfson College, Clare Hall, Fitzwilliam College, Homerton College, Robinson College, Wesley House, Westcott House, Ridley Hall and Westminster College.

Previous page: Bodley's Court, King's College
Right: King's College reflected in the River Cam

CONTENTS

Right: King's College Chapel
Overleaf: The River Cam by King's College

FOREWORD

'All that has clothed with an unfading immortality the name of Newton was produced while this was his 'quiet habitation' and the place of his long and almost uninterrupted abode. And the disciples and friends of Newton all made this the scene of their best and most important labours. It was here that they pondered and discovered, that they went from page to page and from thought to thought. Our walls have been conscious of their soliloquies. Their walks are the paths where we still roam. Their books are in our hands. Our hearths have been consecrated by their presence. We tread upon ground hallowed by their thoughtful steps, amid the same reverend forms of tower and grove which met their contemplative eyes. And if the moonbeams or the night breezes as they touch our battlements can still minister to us a calmness of repose, and refresh our spirits from the intensity of thought or the turmoil of daily life; can we refrain from imagining that they also must have felt these soothing and kindly influences mingle with their high thoughts, and that the workings of their great minds may have been tinged and pervaded by the unseen spirit of the place which still lingers around us?'

William Whewell, 1794-1866
From a sermon preached in Trinity College Chapel,
December 17, 1828

Left: Trinity viewed from St John's chapel tower

SETTING THE SCENE

Cambridge has played a significant part in civilisation for over two thousand years. In England's history of successive invasions its influential position was recognised by Romans, Danes and Normans alike. Nothing now remains of any castle on the steep, man-made mound that overlooks the town, with its all important river crossing at the foot of Castle Hill, but the climb brings its rewards. The soft-toned stonework of the city spread below evokes a sense of timelessness, and the skyline is crowned with elegant outlines of churches and college chapels. The irenic centre of Cambridge is mercifully unscarred by modern high-rise intrusions, even though an occasional upstart tower block on the outskirts now dares to compete with its central superiors. The pervading calm, praised by poets through the ages, continues to inspire citizens, visitors and scholars.

Cambridge may set the scene for reflective thought, but this tranquillity has suffered frequent interruptions. Even when the threat of war subsided, medieval times saw the devastating onslaught of the 'Black Death'. Ironically, plague provoked the creation of several colleges, founded to replace learned men lost to the disease. Cambridge's intellectual status made it the focus of many political and religious upheavals. Henry VIII's sweeping reforms, and the subsequent backlash of religious purging by his daughter, Mary Tudor, radically shaped the town's fortunes. There are harrowing tales of 'heretics' burned at the stake on Midsummer Common, and the town centre itself fell victim to the flames in Cambridge's 'Great Fire' in 1849. Oliver Cromwell found many Royalist adversaries here, and few colleges escaped the ravages of his fanatical assistant, William Dowsing, who was sent to destroy their 'superstitious' Catholic imagery.

From its outset in 1209, the University has sparked its own conflicts. Cambridge's infamous friction between 'Town and Gown' persists through the ages. The fortress-like gates of the ancient colleges were often needed to keep angry commoners at bay when resentment of the University's privileges escalated into violence and destruction. Today a symbiotic arrangement exists: rents from premises in the town assist the University in the costly upkeep of its buildings, while Cambridge commerce relies heavily on income generated by the 31 colleges. Time will never stand still in Cambridge, for its University represents the cutting edge of human advancement. And through it all the life-blood of the city, the river Cam, flows on. This river, which until the 1600's allowed seafaring ships to bring trade to the city, established Cambridge's early wealth. Today the beauty of the river itself is the treasure: for no visit to the town could be complete without experiencing the famous Cambridge punt.

Right: King's Great Gate

A Cambridge

1209 Scholars arrive from Oxford
1284 Peterhouse founded by Bishop Hugh de Balsham
1326 University Hall refounded as Clare College
1347 Pembroke College
1348 Gonville Hall
1350 Trinity Hall
1352 Corpus Christi founded by townspeople
1428 Benedictine monks' hostel created: Buckingham College
1441 King's College endowed by Henry VI
1446 Foundation stone of King's Chapel laid by Henry VI
1448 St Bernard's College refounded as Queen's College
1473 St Catharine's College
1496 Jesus College founded
1505 God's House refounded as Christ's College
1511 St John's College
1542 Buckingham College refounded as Magdalene College
1546 Trinity College founded by Henry VIII
1584 Emmanuel College
1596 Sidney Sussex
1730 Senate House complete

University Timeline

1762	1st Botanic Garden founded
1800	Downing College
1816	Fitzwilliam Museum founded
1829	1st Oxford vs Cambridge Boat Race
1846	Botanic Garden relocated to Trumpington Road
1869	Girton College: the 1st women's college
1871	Newnham College, the 2nd college for women
1882	Selwyn College
1885	Hughes Hall
1896	St Edmund's
1934	University Library designed by Sir Giles Gilbert Scott
1954	New Hall
1960	Churchill College
1964	Darwin College
1965	Clare Hall, Lucy Cavendish & Wolfson College
1966	Fitzwilliam College formally constituted
1976	Homerton College formally adopted into the University
1979	Robinson College: the latest, and 31st, college
2008	New Hall becomes Murray Edwards College
2009	800th Anniversary of Cambridge University

Trinity Great Court

PETERHOUSE

Bishop Hugo de Balsham founded Peterhouse, the first Cambridge college, in 1284. He needed to resolve difficulties that had arisen for his new, secular scholars, who had initially lodged alongside brethren in charge of the Hospital of St John. Their differences were too great, however. Friction arose from the bishop's aim to emulate the principles of Walter de Merton at Oxford, who 'sought to attract the most capable men of all classes, and so to raise up secular schools'. Only two years later Bishop Balsham died, bequeathing funds with which his scholars acquired land and built their hall. However, more than one century elapsed before scholars desperately entreated the Bishop of Ely, John de Fordham, 'the revenue of our house is so small that it barely sufficeth in these days for the support of a Master and fourteen scholars ... nor are our buildings finished, or properly furnished with the necessary offices'. They were granted the Rectory of Hinton, and by 1431 the development of the college was well underway. But a storm of political and religious upheaval lay ahead, and the college would require all the skill of its Masters.

The Whittle Building was opened by HRH the Prince of Wales in January 2015

A spacious deer park extends down to the fen. In the early days, watercourses allowed the visiting bishops of Ely to alight beside the wall and enter through the gate, which is now closed up (below). It bears the crests of 2 bishops of Ely: John Hotham, (between 1316-37), and on the other side, Bishop Alcock, (between 1486-1500). Deer graced the park until the 1930s, when they died out, but these exceptional grounds hold other delights today. Spring reveals glorious displays of daffodils which outshine any other Cambridge garden (overleaf).

Peterhouse chapel is affectionately referred to as the 'Grandfather Clock'

Matthew Wren, uncle of Sir Christopher, the architect, became Master in 1625. Caught in the tides of political change, he was imprisoned by Oliver Cromwell for 18 years. He is remembered as an admirable leader, who introduced many improvements. At that time the college used the neighbouring church, St Mary the Less. Wren commissioned a new chapel which was consecrated on March 17, 1632. The decoration and interior fittings, however, were later completed by Bishop Cosin, who outraged the Puritans by introducing an opulent luxury, incense, during services.

In the 16th century, Master Andrew Perne's strategy to survive turbulent religious change was controversial. Perne had no tolerance for 'the names of partialities, sects or divisions, either in civil or religious causes' which he viewed as 'but foolish words or petting terms'. Thus he simply adopted the view of the moment, switching allegiances as needed to ensure the security of his college, not to mention himself. This provoked his disenchanted University peers to create a new Latin verb, *pernare*, meaning to change often. He is described as 'a morning book-worm and afternoon malt-worm, a right juggler, as full of his sleights, wiles, fetches, casts of leger-de-main, toys to mock apes withal, odd shifts and knavish practises as his skin can hold'.

Peterhouse is associated with many great scientists. The brilliant Henry Cavendish, who first recognised hydrogen gas as a distinct substance, attended in the mid 1700s. He was an exceedingly shy person, who refused to have his portrait painted. Luckily, as a gentleman, he was spared the trauma of having to take any oral examination. Eminent physicist Lord Kelvin was a fellow here. In 1884, to mark the college's 600th anniversary, he made Peterhouse the first college to receive electric lighting. This did not receive unanimous approval, as the local laundresses were enraged by the smuts from the generator, which spoiled their washing. Christopher Cockerell, inventor of the hovercraft, was also a fellow. The jet inventor, Sir Frank Whittle, and 'father of the computer', Charles Babbage, were both students here.

Peterhouse today is dedicated to 'the advancement of education, religion, learning and research'. It welcomes students of diverse backgrounds and aims to honour Hugo de Balsham's original purpose, 'to introduce scholars in the schools, who are to live together and study in the University of Cambridge; to dwell in the same College forever, and employ themselves with appropriate study, to the praise of God and the perpetual augmentation of the same university'.

Right: Massed daffodils of Peterhouse's 'deer park'

CLARE

Clare College, founded in 1326 as University Hall by Richard de Badew, now takes its name from Edward I's granddaughter Lady Elizabeth de Clare, whose financial intervention in 1338 saved the foundation. She turned to charitable works having been widowed three times; golden tears on the black border of her insignia allude to her bereavement. This was an era of terrible visitations of plague, and Lady Elizabeth intended to help replace the hundreds of clergy who were 'taken away by the fangs of pestilence'. Even with her contribution the college struggled at times: thirty or so members at one point shared two chairs, one jug and two basins. Disaster struck in 1521 when fire destroyed many early documents and treasures; in 1548 it narrowly escaped amalgamation with Trinity Hall thanks to the intercession of religious reformer Nicholas Ridley.

By the beginning of the 17th century, Clare's dilapidated original buildings were in need of replacement. The fellows wished to relocate their buildings further from the street and wanted recreational use of the river bank, so they set out to acquire an area of land belonging to neighbouring King's College. Eagerly they procured a royal mandate instructing King's to grant the land, before actually consulting with their neighbour. This prompted a series of acrimonious exchanges disputing matters such as overshadowing and privacy, not to mention 'ye annoyance of ye windes gathering between ye Chappell and our Colledge', before a royal letter settled the matter in favour of Clare.

Happily, this ruling resulted in a harmonious set of buildings 'more like a palace than a college' Although it might appear they were all constructed contemporaneously, Clare's renovation took place over 77 years from 1638-1715. The south range was completed by 1642, but the later west range, was hindered by Cromwell requisitioning the stone to reinforce Cambridge castle. Architects James Essex and James Burrough may have contributed to the design, but is unlikely that Inigo Jones played a part, as the college once liked to believe. The elegant chapel was consecrated in 1769. Inside, ethereal light from the lantern tower evokes an air of spiritual calm. Cipriani's beautiful Annunciation, above the altar, and the 1863 stained glass window representing Lady Elizabeth, complete the chapel's beauty.

Clare College was closely linked with the turbulence of the Tudor Court. Notable for his morality, diplomacy and eloquence, Hugh Latimer was elected a Fellow in 1510. His sympathies with religious reform earned him the honour of being appointed royal chaplain to Henry VIII and Anne Boleyn. Latimer was instrumental in the dissolution of the monasteries, for which he paid dearly when Henry's vengeful daughter, Mary Tudor, had him burned at the stake in Oxford in 1555.

Left: Clare's crest, displayed on ornate wrought iron gates
Right: High Summer in Clare's elegant Front Court

Clare is rightly renowned for its beautiful stone bridge, which was the main priority in 1638 when rebuilding commenced. A favourite Cambridge challenge is to invite visitors to count the stone balls adorning it. The answer is not 14, as it first appears, but 13 4/5. Several tales surround the reason for the mysterious missing segment, the most popular theory being revenge by builder, Thomas Grumbold. The college paid him a mere three shillings for his work; thus he ensured that the bridge would never be truly completed. The bridge provides an unrivalled view of the Backs, which was listed as a Grade 1 Historic Park in 1995.

Clare inspires creative thinking. The elegant balustrades around the roof line of Old Court once proved too tempting to imaginative students, who used over a mile of string to construct a giant spider's web, complete with a spider, named Arabella. Further creativity may be enjoyed at the college each summer, when students stage Shakespeare plays in the gardens. Drama is a tradition that dates back many centuries. In James I's time, the college staged a fine example of Town and Gown rivalry in *Club Law*: a parody of the town's dignitaries. With the aim of maximum provocation, townspeople were invited and then 'riveted in with scholars on all sides' to endure the spectacle. King James himself so enjoyed the college's production of another parody, *The Ignoramus*, that he came to see it twice.

In 1947, after World War 2, Clare's famous gardens were redesigned by E.N. Willner. Blends of light and shade, geometry and natural forms, create a living palette of colour in vibrant herbaceous borders. The gardens offer delightful vistas of Clare's buildings and King's Chapel. In Spring, a profusion of daffodils brightens the shady avenue.

In 1926 Clare extended beyond Queen's Road, building Memorial Court, which was designed by Sir Giles Gilbert-Scott. In 1972 it was among the first three Cambridge colleges to become coeducational. Seven hundred years after Lady Elizabeth's first statutes, it still 'sendeth forth its students, who have tasted of its sweetness, ... to rise to diverse heights according to the claim of their deserts'.

A statue of Confucius (right), standing in the Avenue, symbolises the college's strong links with Chinese culture and history. As early as 1685, Nathaniel Vincent, a member of the college, produced the first English translations of Confucius' teachings

Clare's illustrious alumni include the composer, John Rutter, renowned naturalist Sir David Attenborough, and James Watson, who in 2005 unveiled a sculpture of the Double Helix in Memorial Court to commemorate his 1953 co-discovery of the structure of DNA.

PEMBROKE

Marie de Saint Pol, Countess of Pembroke, was a close friend of Elizabeth de Clare, who may have inspired Marie to create this, Cambridge's third oldest college, in 1347. Like the Lady Elizabeth, she was ill fated in marriage, widowed after only three years. Marie was daughter of Guy de Châtillon, Comte de St Pol, in France. Thus she is referred to in Thomas Gray's poem, where her husband's untimely death is romanticised as occurring in a jousting tournament on his wedding day,

'... sad Châtillon, on her bridal morn
That wept her bleeding love.'

The countess herself lived for 30 years after her college's foundation. She demonstrated great wisdom in providing all the facilities it needed to operate independently, including Cambridge's first collegiate chapel. Pembroke soon earned a reputation for good character and learning. Queen Elizabeth I visited in 1564, and was impressed, exclaiming *O domus antiqua et religiosa!* (O ancient and devout house!).

Pembroke enjoyed a long period of stability. By the 1870s however, rising student numbers prompted the college to ask architect Alfred Waterhouse to devise 'the best way of providing for the College a group of buildings as efficient, convenient and architecturally effective as the site was capable of'. Waterhouse's enthusiastic response called for a total rebuild, including demolition of Wren's chapel. His designs for a new Master's lodge, hall and library went ahead, along with Red Buildings: a departure from traditional Cambridge stonework with its red brick and French Renaissance style tower. In 1878, however, the college prudently consulted Sir George Gilbert Scott instead, which saved the chapel and old library, and created New Court in 1881.

Marie's original chapel was later converted into a library. Dr Matthew Wren was a fellow of Pembroke, but also Master of Peterhouse. While imprisoned by Oliver Cromwell in the Tower of London he vowed to create a chapel for Pembroke, should he ever be free again. He commissioned his nephew, Sir Christopher Wren, and the building (above) was consecrated in 1665. Sir George Gilbert Scott's extension to the chapel, including splendid Italian marble columns, was consecrated in 1881.

William Pitt the Younger came to Pembroke in 1773, aged only fourteen. Ten years later he became Britain's youngest ever Prime Minister, emulating his father, William Pitt the Elder, who held the position himself for two years. Pitt might not be thanked by some for introducing Britain's first income tax, but his skill in foreign affairs is unquestionable. His involvement in the Third Coalition against France led to the famous defeat of the French at the Battle of Trafalgar in 1805.

Pembroke is recounted by many as a haven of peace. In 1524 religious reformer Nicholas Ridley accepted election as a fellow here in preference to a similar offer from University College, Oxford. He became Pembroke's Master in 1540. He worked with Thomas Cranmer to bring about the Reformation, and assisted Cranmer's compilation of The Book of Common Prayer. For years he skilfully deflected accusations of heresy, but was finally arrested when he went to beg Queen Mary's pardon after his involvement in Lady Jane Grey's failed claim to the throne. He was burned at the stake in Oxford on 16th October 1555. In a final message to his beloved college he writes,

> *'Farewell, Pembroke Hall, of late mine own college, my cure, and my charge ... In thy orchard (the walls, buts, and trees, if they could hear me speak, would bear me witness), I learned without book almost all Paul's Epistles'.*

Pembroke's grounds today form a series of intimate gardens which include an abundantly planted herbaceous border along the path commemoratively named Ridley's Walk. The college has been home to many creative individuals, including poets Edmund Spenser, Thomas Gray and Ted Hughes. Gray moved to Pembroke after an unhappy time at Peterhouse: his letter dated 25th March 1756 explains,

> *'I left my lodgings because the rooms were noisy, and the People of the house dirty ... All I shall say more is, that I am for the present extremely well lodged here, and as quiet as in the Grand Chartreuse; and that everybody ... are as civil as they could be to Mary de Valence in person'.*

When peace was shattered by World War 1, Pembroke offered use of its buildings to the War Office, and became one of the first Officers' Training Schools. Today, the memorial in the chapel cloister bears the names of 305 members and 3 College servants who sacrificed their lives: a greater loss than at any other Cambridge college.

Right: Ridley's Walk

Caius' design for Gate of Honour is based on Roman tombs he saw during his time in Italy.

GONVILLE & CAIUS

The Gothic tower of Gonville and Caius dominates the end of King's Parade, while carved faces of its bygone fellows watch over Trinity Street. Founded by Edmund Gonville in 1348, the college was originally located behind St Botolph's churchyard: an area now occupied by Corpus Christi. It aimed to instruct scholars 'in dialectic and other sciences'. Edmund died three years later, bequeathing the college to his friend William Bateman, who was then developing his own college, Trinity Hall. In 1353 Bateman relocated Gonville Hall nearer the town centre. Two centuries later, however, the college was in serious decline.

Help came in the form of the eminent physician John Keys, who had studied at the original Gonville Hall. He travelled extensively in Italy, qualifying as a Doctor of Medicine in 1541 at the University of Padua. On returning to England in 1544 he changed his name to the Latinised form of *Caius*. When he came back to Cambridge in 1557 he refounded his *alma mater* as Gonville & Caius College and became its Master in 1559. Six years later, at four o'clock in the morning on the 5th of May 1565, he began renovation of his college. The inscription on the foundation stone is *Johannes Caius posuit sapiente.* (John Caius laid down wisdom) declaring his goal of excellence. He had no tolerance of imperfection: one of his first statutes, (which has long since been deemed quite unacceptable), excluded scholars who were 'deaf, dumb, deformed, lame, confirmed invalids or Welshmen'.

Dr Caius designed three gates to inspire his scholars. Students enter via the Gate of Humility: the proper attitude for learning, and pass daily under the Gate of Virtue. This is adorned with two figures, one holding a palm branch and a wreath, the other a purse and cornucopia: the rewards of diligent study. On Graduation Day students depart triumphantly from the splendid Gate of Honour situated in Senate House Passage.

Opposite: Tree Court was controversially rebuilt by Waterhouse in 1870

The Crick Memorial

Although his original statutes, (107 chapters!) are more concerned with domestic details, Caius' main purpose for his college was medicine. With this in mind he obtained a royal licence allowing dissection of the human body. Although he was physician to both Edward VI and Queen Mary, Queen Elizabeth I dismissed him because of his Catholicism. During 14 years as Master his Catholicism also clashed with Puritan elements of the University, culminating when senior University officials raided his rooms in 1572, and destroyed his beloved Catholic 'College Treasures'. Heartbroken, he died soon afterwards in 1573.

The college today has an excellent reputation for research and the sciences. Past college members include physicist Stephen Hawking, William Harvey, who discovered the circulation of blood, and Sir James Chadwick, discoverer of the neutron. Francis Crick, who worked to define the structure of DNA, is commemorated in a beautiful, symbolic memorial in the path beneath the Great Gate. This was unveiled 25th April 2013 by his colleague, James Watson, marking the 60th anniversary of his ground breaking paper's publication.

Caius has the oldest Cambridge college chapel still in use. It honours the college's leaders with vividly personal memorials. Several windows are dedicated to Masters from the 19th century. However, the most unusual tombs are those of Thomas Legge, successor to Caius, and also Dr Stephen Perse, who are both represented by vibrantly painted figures kneeling in prayer. Most impressive of all is the tomb of Caius himself, for which he gave instructions three weeks before his death: this was erected in 1575. The chapel was repaired in the early 1700s. In 1870, Alfred Waterhouse was commissioned to refurbish the building. He refaced the exterior and extended the east end with an unusual domed, Byzantine style apse. This has been richly decorated with mosaics by Antonio Salviati, depicting biblical scenes of teaching.

A Victorian plaster cast of Dr Caius' skull observes visitors from high on his memorial. The tomb was first disturbed in 1719 during building work, when a witness recounts,
'The body seem'd to have been a very lusty one, and ye coffin was pretty full of it; the fflesh was of a yellowish black colour, and yielded to ye least touch of ye stick and fell to pieces. The eyes sank deep into their sockets. A long grey beard much like that wch we see in ye picture of him, only this was grown very rough by long time: I think it was about 145 years from ye time of his death. I touch'd his beard with ye stick and turn'd it a little on one side; it accordingly lay on one side, having lost all manner of elasticity: I therefore brought it back to its right place again. The sight occasion'd in me serious reflections, and I went away with such a regard as I thought due to ye memory of so considerable a mann as Dr Caius had been.'"

Left: The College courtyards are enhanced with expert planting of bright flowers throughout the year

TRINITY HALL

The Black Death affected all levels of society indiscriminately. In 1350 it had wiped out 700 of Bishop William Bateman's clergy in Norfolk and Suffolk, and he sought to remedy matters. Three years earlier John de Crauden had given him a monks' hostel in Cambridge, which he chose to become Trinity Hall. Bateman intended more than replacement of his priests. He wanted to train logicians and lawyers who could support papal authority, and stipulated that a minimum of ten out of the twenty fellows should be secular. It has remained a stronghold for the legal profession. Lord Chesterfield referred to Trinity Hall as 'the best in all the University' and 'full of lawyers who have lived in the world and know how to behave'.

The college's name has sometimes been understandably confused with Trinity College. Its history relates to the days when college meant the body of people at the establishment, and hall referred to the building: hence the early names Clare Hall, King's Hall etc. By the time this trend had begun to change, Henry VIII had already founded Trinity College, so Trinity Hall had to remain unaltered. The buildings themselves have altered significantly: the medieval brickwork was largely refaced in 1745, and the east range was rebuilt by Salvin in 1852, after a fire. The chapel, the smallest in Cambridge or Oxford, remains largely unchanged since its refurbishment in 1730.

Trinity Hall escaped the worst of Cambridge's religious and political conflict. It has been described as a place of 'unadventurous stability'. Nonetheless its alumni include former Prime Ministers of Australia, Burma and Pakistan, former Deputy Prime Minister Geoffrey Howe, novelist J.B. Priestley, and United Nations leader Hans Blix. It is also renowned for its sporting success, especially in rowing: Olympic medallists Tom James and Emma Pooley both studied here.

Trinity Hall's distinctive crest may be seen elsewhere around town on milestones, which were erected between Cambridge and London in 1730. These were the first milestones since Roman times, and were funded by Dr William Mowse for the benefit of the lawyers, who frequently travelled to the capital.

The Jerwood Library

Trinity Hall's Elizabethan library, erected in 1590, is one of the oldest in Cambridge. In accordance with Bishop Bateman's original instructions, certain books are still chained. The curious door high up in the wall once opened on to a walkway connecting to the old Master's lodge. The Jerwood Library, built in 1998, is a striking feature of the Backs. Designed by Freeland Rees Roberts, its award-winning modern design merges subtly with the adjoining historic buildings.

The college gardens are a miniature jewel in Cambridge's crown of horticultural splendour. They have recently been redesigned following the regretful removal of the ancient chestnut trees, which succumbed to disease. In the 1770s, Dr Jowett created 'a pretty little fairy garden, with narrow walks besprinkled with shells and pellucid pebbles, and enclosed by a Chinese railing'. A poem by Dr Mansell records,

'A little garden, little Jowett made.
And fenced it with a little palisade;
If you would know the taste of little Jowett,
This little garden won't a little show it'

Dr Jowett is accredited with the composition of the chimes for Great St Mary's church, which have since become famous as the *Westminster Chimes* of Big Ben.

The original Elizabethan Library

Right: Venerable Beech tree on Latham Lawn
Overleaf: Trinity Hall and Clare Bridge

CORPUS CHRISTI

Cambridge's frequent visitations of plague devastated the population, and the town especially felt the loss of its priests. In 1352 the city guilds of Corpus Christi and the Blessed Virgin Mary united to create a college – the only one to be founded by the town. An impression of the college's early appearance may be gained in Free School Lane, where tiny windows are set in rough clunch walls, darkened with soot. Its location by St Bene't's church gave rise to the name Bene't's College, by which it was familiarly known for about 200 years after the Reformation. A bridge, still extant, connects the college to the church, and there is a small window where activity in the chapel can be observed. However, only 30 years passed before the town turned on its own creation. In 1381, Corpus Christi bore the brunt of the Peasants' Revolt, for the college was despised as a harsh landlord. Many parchments and treasures were stolen and burned in the market place. An old woman named Margaret Sterr is said to have thrown the ashes in the air crying, 'Thus, thus let the learning of all scholars be confounded'. The College persisted regardless. Discipline was severe. In 1573 a rule was imposed requiring Latin to be spoken at all times during Full Term, and errant students would be 'subject to the heaviest penalties for speaking English'.

Matthew Parker studied at Corpus Christi and was ordained in 1527. He became chaplain to Henry VIII, who recommended him to become Master in 1544. Parker taught Henry's daughter Elizabeth, who appointed him as Archbishop of Canterbury in 1559, soon after she became queen. During his studies to prove the origins of a Christian Church in England which was independent from the Catholic Church in Rome, he amassed a magnificent collection of books and manuscripts which he presented to the college. This treasure, which includes the sixth-century Gospel Book of St Augustine, and the original manuscript of the Anglo-Saxon Chronicle of the late ninth century, still ranks as one of the finest libraries in the world. Parker well knew it, and safeguarded his treasure by instructing that if a certain number of books or manuscripts were missing at the end of the year the whole gift should go to Caius College, and if they were similarly careless, on to Trinity Hall. Corpus Christi has proved a worthy custodian, since 400 years later the collection is still complete.

Marlowe's memorial

Christopher Marlowe studied here between 1580 and 1587. He was a leading playwright and poet whose black comedy, 'The Jew of Malta', may have inspired Shakespeare's Shylock. He was also involved in espionage, and was reportedly stabbed to death, aged just 29.

A portrait discovered at the college in 1953, consistent with Marlowe's age and dates, has since been proved not to be him.

Corpus Chapel's flawless design is enhanced by immaculate lawns.

Old Court

Old Court, with its mellow plaster work and narrow windows, is Cambridge's oldest surviving medieval court. Troubled ghosts are said to linger here. In the 1630s, when plague struck yet again, the Master Dr Henry Butts bravely stayed to tend the stricken townsfolk. In desperate solitude he wrote, 'alone, a destitute and forsaken man; not a Scholler with me in the College, not a Scholler seen by me without'. The horror drove him to hang himself on Easter Sunday, in 1632.

The college used St Bene't's church until 1579, when their first chapel was built. However, this did not improve its general antiquated appearance: in 1710 the bibliographer Uffenbach condemned it as 'one of the ugliest colleges'. Its face changed dramatically in the 1820s, when William Wilkins created the elegant Gothic façade of New Court. He was so pleased with his design that he chose to be buried in the chapel.

The college emblem is the pelican, which was said to have offered its own blood to feed its children. It symbolises self-sacrifice in the form of the body and blood of Christ. This theme has inspired several beautiful works of art within the college.

The Corpus Clock was unveiled by physicist Stephen Hawking on 19th September 2008, and has since commanded an almost constant audience on the corner of Bene't Street. It was conceived and funded by Dr John C Taylor, and constructed near Cambridge in the Huxley Bertram workshops. It features six new patented inventions, but the design also pays homage to 18th century English horologist John Harrison, who invented the grasshopper escapement clock mechanism. Dr Taylor's clock has been built inside out to reveal this impressive spring-driven clockwork mechanism.

'He'll eat up every minute of your life, and as soon as one has gone he's salivating for the next'. Dr John C Taylor

The sinister grasshopper-like creature, sculpted by Matthew Sanderson, is called a Chronophage (time eater). Its jaws gnaw constantly at time, and every 15 minutes it raises its sting menacingly. You may see it blink at random. Every 60 minutes it opens its jaws wide, gorging itself, while stinging the hour to death to the sound of a chain rattling into a wooden coffin. As the feeding frenzy subsides it shudders with satisfaction before the grating sound of the 'daily grind' resumes. The clock has an unsettling, irregular movement. The pendulum sometimes pauses, and the blue LEDs flash first slowly, then chase as if to catch up. The clock reads accurately every five minutes, fluctuating in between.

The gold-plated disc was shaped by forcing a sheet of steel into a mould using a controlled explosive charge. Electricity is used solely for the winding mechanism, and lighting the LEDs which are arranged in concentric circles displaying the time in hours, minutes and seconds. The warning inscription below is Matthew Parker's own motto, from Vulgate, 1 John, 2:17. It reads *Mundus transit et concupiscentia eius* (The world passeth away, and the lust thereof).

Magdalene's magnificent Wisteria

MAGDALENE

Magdalene College, by the site of Cambridge's original Great Bridge, is the only ancient college set entirely on the far side of the river. It was founded as Monks' Hostel in 1428, so named because it housed Benedictine student monks. However, by 1483 it had become known as Buckingham College, and the Dukes of Buckingham had funded much of its early development. A change came in 1539 when the affiliated abbey at Croyland surrendered to Henry VIII. In 1542 the king gave the college to his Lord Chancellor, Thomas Audley. This ruthless man had presided over the trial of Bishop John Fisher, who dared to oppose the king's first divorce. Audley refounded the college as Magdalene College, which he ordered to be spelled *Maudleyn*, to include his name. When he died, only two years later, it was said of his gravestone that 'The stone is not harder, nor the marble blacker, than the heart of him who lies beneath'. The college evolved slowly: the Duke of Norfolk promised £40 per annum in 1564 to complete its quadrangle, and Sir Christopher Wray contributed further funding around 1585. Magdalene's Master at this time was the unpopular Degory Nichols, whose wife's scolding voice could be heard all over the college. He was succeeded in 1582 by Thomas Nevile, who presided for nine years before taking over at Trinity College.

Many buildings around Quayside belong to Magdalene; the area was rebuilt between 1982 and 1989. At this time a gargoyle was added on the river wall facing the college. This depicts the Genoese banker, Benedict Spinola who, in 1575, embezzled the college by developing and selling on land which had been bequeathed by Thomas Audley. Magdalene's finances suffered disastrously, and it pursued legal actions in vain. More than 400 years later it remembers its old adversary in this caricature designed by Peter Fluck and Roger Law: the creators of 'Spitting Image'. Here he is condemned to forever dribble water into the Cam as 'Revenge at last!'

Samuel Pepys entered the college as a student in 1650, but his diary mentions subsequent visits. Sunday 26th February 1659 recounts,

> *'By and by, Mr. Pechell and Sanchy and I went out, Pechell to Church, Sanchy and I to the Rose Tavern, where we sat and drank till sermon done, and then Mr Pechell came to us, and we three sat drinking the King's and his whole family's health till it began to be dark'*

Pepys himself donated £60 towards the building which still houses his magnificent collection of books, bequeathed to the college "for the sake of my own and nephew's education therein". The building was begun during the mastership of Dr Pechell, and the books were received in 1724: this date is inscribed on the building below Pepys' motto *Mens cujusque is est quisque* (The mind is the man).

The Pepys Library

Pepys would have been disappointed to return in the later 1700s for, especially due to the influence of William Farish, Magdalene had become known as a fervent centre of Evangelical thought. Pepys, ever the bon viveur, would have found no ale or wine to refresh him. The river is said to have been rendered 'unnavigable with tea leaves', and Magdalene students were referred to in the town as 'The Saints'.

Magdalene's motto is *Garde ta foy* (Keep your faith), and the college has strong associations with men of religious conviction, including three Archbishops of Canterbury: Thomas Cranmer, and Michael Ramsey (1961-1974). A.C. Benson, who became Master in 1915, was son of Archbishop Edward White Benson (1882-96). The current Master is once more a former Archbishop of Canterbury: Dr Rowan Williams took up the position in January 2013. Professor of English, and author of the *Narnia Chronicles*, C.S. Lewis, became a Fellow in 1953, and spent the last ten years of his life here.

As the college expanded in the 1900s it extended across Magdalene Street to incorporate a collection of buildings which are today known as The Village. Here, the varied architecture of Benson Court includes a beamed Tudor house, a former vinegar factory, and the Lutyens Building, completed in 1932 by Edwin Lutyens. Mallory Court commemorates mountaineer George Mallory, who perished in his attempt to climb Mount Everest in 1924. Further college members have included film director Mike Newell, who created *Harry Potter and the Goblet of Fire*, actor Sir Michael Redgrave and also the inspired horticulturist Monty Don. Irish leader C.S. Parnell, and television journalist John Simpson also studied here. Dr Loyd Grossman who, besides his fame as a food critic, is a major patron of historical organisations, received his PhD at Magdalene. The College has a slightly more traditional feel than many other Colleges and still has formal dinners in the beautiful candle-lit hall. It retained the University's all-male tradition until 1988, when it became the last College to become co-educational. Today, Magdalene's academic reputation goes from strength to strength.

Above: Mallory Court
Right: The Lutyens Building

KING'S

King's College Chapel projects an aura of regal dignity over the town, and its outline, dominating the Backs, is Cambridge's defining image. King Henry VI was 19 when he set out his stipulations for the building '...in large fourme clene and substancial, settying a parte superfluite of too gret curious werkes of entaille and besy moulding'. He laid the chapel foundation stone on St James' Day, July 25th 1446. However, preparations for 'The King's College of St Nicholas' had already begun five years earlier, in 1441. In order to accommodate his ambitious plans a considerable site had to be acquired: this led to serious disruption of the town's main trading area.

The king planned in minute detail ranging from the dimensions of buildings to projected wages of the workforce, but in fact little of his original scheme came into being. Henry would have built the chapel to enclose the northern side of the main quadrangle, with a gate central to the east side, and chambers to the south. A lecture room with a library above would have completed the west side. He intended a burial ground surrounded by a cloister, a 120 foot high belfry, and a garden 'for to sette in certain trees and floures behoueful and conuenient for the service of the chirche'. He envisaged the whole site enclosed by a high wall with towers at intervals, creating a forest of turrets arranged so that each occupied its own space in the scene, with no interference from the others. The chapel spires would have been the crowning glory.

Henry's other college, 'our Royal foundation of St Mary at Eton' was developing simultaneously and he decided to 'weld the two colleges together in an everlasting brotherhood'. Thus his Cambridge foundation became 'The King's College of Our Lady and St Nicholas in Cambridge'.

Previous page: Cows still graze on Scholars' Piece by the Chapel
Left: King's Screen goes some way to creating Henry's original vision of massed turrets complementing the Chapel

The Great Gate

King's screen and Great Gate were designed by William Wilkins, who beat 18 competing architects to the honour in 1823. It is richly adorned with the Tudor insignia of roses, crowns and portcullises, and the elegant latticed windows cast a tracery of shadow on the immaculate lawns lining King's Parade.

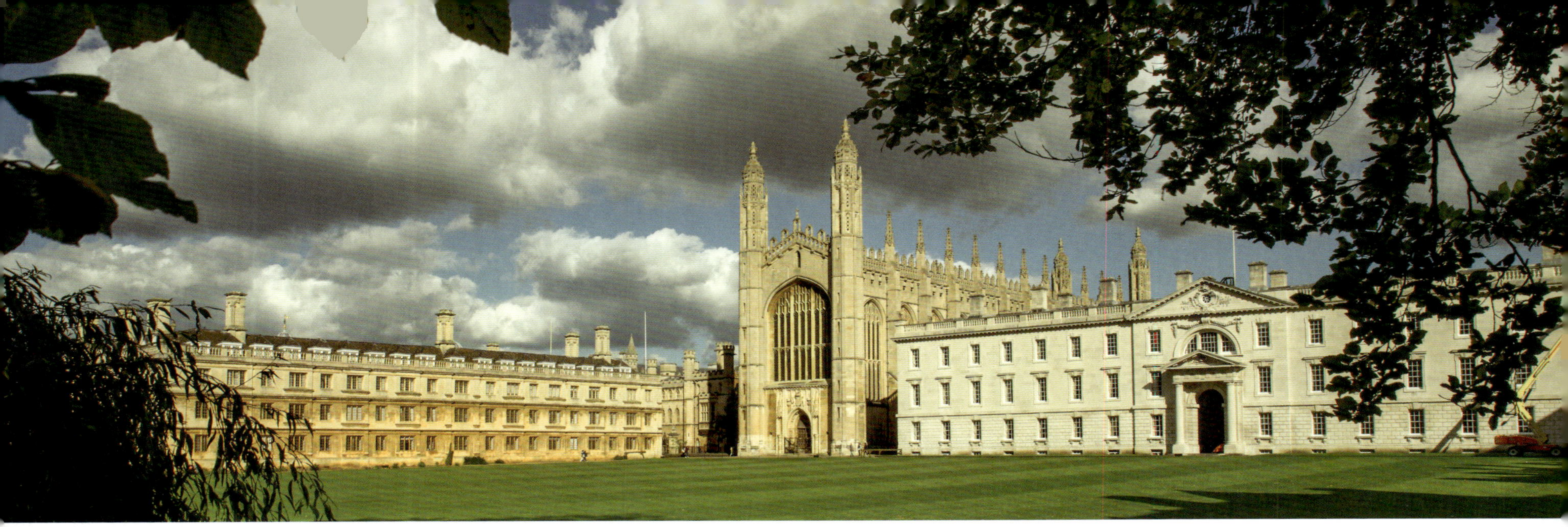

Tragically, Henry would never see his design completed. In 1461 work on the chapel was abruptly abandoned when he was defeated by Edward of York. A partially cut stone was left lying on the college green until 1724, when it was chosen as the foundation stone for the Fellows' Building. However, four further kings ensured completion of the chapel. Edward IV contributed a little, and Richard III built most of the main structure between 1483 and 1485, but was killed by Henry VII at the battle of Bosworth. When Henry VII visited Cambridge 21 years later in 1506 he realised the chapel's symbolic significance, as the population still revered Henry VI as a saint. To support his great work would win public approval, so by 1508 building had resumed in earnest, installing the opulent interior stonework. Master mason, John Wastell, created the glorious fan vaulted ceiling in only three years. By 1515 the stone structure was finished, leaving Henry VIII to add the organ screen, stalls and windows, which were completed by 1536.

Twenty five of the chapel windows portray 'the story of the olde and newe law', while the east end depicts the crucifixion. The vibrant colours and expressive individuality of the figures make each image a work of art in its own right. The windows miraculously survived Cromwell's reign, possibly because the college paid 6s, 8d to appease Cromwell's henchman, William Dowsing. Even so, the glass was at great risk from Cromwell's soldiers, who used the chapel as a stable. The west window was created by Clayton and Bell in 1879. In WW2 all the glass but the east window was removed and hidden. Repair of the chapel has occasionally been required: in 1765 high winds dislodged a pinnacle which plummeted four feet deep into the earth, narrowly missing passers-by. In 1961, when A.E. Allnatt gave the magnificent painting, Rubens' *The Adoration of the Magi*, the floor behind the altar was specially lowered to fit it below the window. This painting suffered shocking vandalism in 1974, when it was defaced with the initials IRA.

Above: The grey Portland stone Fellows' Building, by James Gibbs, was begun in 1724

Bodley's Court

The chapel's admirers include Joseph Haydn, who enthusiastically described it in a letter to Beethoven. Saint Säens complimented the 'admirable choristers', and Yehudi Menuhin performed a charity concert here in 1965. Over 50,000 people visit the chapel every year, but a spiritual calm prevails over the thronging crowds. Each Christmas it broadcasts worldwide the Festival of Nine Lessons and Carols: a tradition begun in 1928 when this was the historic first live BBC radio broadcast. Before the opening procession, one choirboy is selected to sing the first verse of *Once in Royal David's City* as a solo, before the full choir takes up the song. Wordsworth's sonnet vividly describes:

But, from the arms of silence - list! O list!
The music bursteth into second life;
The notes luxuriate, every stone is kissed
By sound, or ghost of sound, in mazy strife;
Heart-thrilling strains, that cast, before the eye
Of the devout, a veil of ecstasy!

For centuries, King's remained exclusively a college for Etonians. From the outset, the students enjoyed special privileges. They could claim a degree without taking an examination, nor were they answerable to the University proctors. As early as 1454, jealous members of other colleges felt provoked to attack them 'with guns and habiliments of war'. The college's insular existence led to a somewhat indolent reputation, but a college revival began in the 1820s, when new annual examinations ended the luxury of a 'free degree'. In 1865 the first non-Etonian students were admitted. At this time the college expanded, with the Chetwynd Building by Sir Giles Gilbert Scott added to Wilkins' range of buildings on the south side; in 1893 Bodley's Court was completed.

In 1871 King's also began to accept non-Anglicans. After WW2, the 'Nonconformist' trend continued when students from outside the conventional Oxbridge background were encouraged. In 1973 King's was among the first colleges to admit women as undergraduates.

King's Bridge was relocated to this position in 1818

King's punts

King's alumni include Francis Walsingham, who matriculated in 1548, and later became advisor and 'spy master' to Queen Elizabeth I. Britain's first Prime Minister, Robert Walpole entered the college in 1696. At the turn of the 20th century, King's was closely associated with the Bloomsbury Group which included economist John Maynard Keynes, who went on to become King's Bursar and transformed the fortunes of the college. Poet Rupert Brooke also studied here and became a Fellow in 1913. Fifty years earlier, his father had been the first non-Etonian Fellow to be elected at King's. Novelist E.M. Forster was a student between 1897 and 1901, and later took residence at the college after he became an Honorary Fellow in 1946.

The mathematical genius Alan Turing, who devised the means of deciphering German WW2 messages generated by the Enigma machine, studied at King's between 1931 and 1934. He later became a Fellow of the college before working at Bletchley Park. More recent members include Polish children's book designer and author, Jan Pieńkowski, and the journalist and politician Martin Bell.

King's has strong links with China. The Chinese poet, Xú Zhìmó, was a graduate student in the 1920s. His poem On Leaving Cambridge was written in 1928, three years before his untimely death in a plane crash. Today it is widely taught in Chinese schools. The first and last lines are inscribed on the white Beijing marble Chinese Stone, which was installed in 2008 by the river, source of the poet's inspiration.

Quietly I take my leave
Just as quietly as I came;
Softly I wave a farewell
To the clouds in the western sky

Silently I am going
As silently as I came
Tenderly I wave my sleeve
Lest I disturb a speck of cloud.

Above: The Gibbs Building
Right: King's College Chapel

QUEENS'

'Indeed, as Miltiades' trophy in Athens would not suffer Thermistocles to sleep, so this Queen, beholding her husband's bounty in building King's College, was restless in herself with holy emulation until she had produced something of the like nature'.

Margaret of Anjou, young wife of King Henry VI, soon brought about her ambition, 'to laud and honneure of sexe feminine'. In 1448, two years after her husband began King's chapel, Andrew Dokett persuaded her to support his idea for a new project. Dokett had founded his own college, St Bernard's, in 1446, but wanted to tempt the queen with the idea of creating a splendid 'Queen's College' to sit alongside King's. When Margaret obtained her letters patent on April 15th 1448 Dokett's original foundation became the College of St Margaret and St Bernard. He proceeded to build Old Court and the Great Gate; the red brick buildings by the river were constructed soon afterwards, in the 1450s.

When Henry VI was overthrown, Dokett hastened to find favour with the new queen, Elizabeth Woodville. She consented to be named as co-foundress, and the college's first proper statutes were issued on 10th March 1475. Thus the college's origins are due to the generosity of more than one queen, signified by the all-important apostrophe in its name. However, this did not officially move from Queen's to Queens' until 1831. The college gained further royal favour when Lady Margaret Beaufort stayed there in 1505 while her advisor, Bishop John Fisher, was President. Katharine of Aragon visited in 1521, and also her husband, King Henry VIII, in 1522. In 1949, the Queen Mother, Elizabeth Bowes-Lyon became patroness, followed by our own Queen Elizabeth II.

The President's Lodge, built around 1460

The red brick and wooden beams of Queens' distinguish its architecture amongst the Cambridge colleges. For many years the timbers of Cloister Court were plastered over, but these were rediscovered in 1923. When Erasmus became Professor of Greek between 1511 and 1513, he occupied the tower in the south west corner of the court (opposite), where his top floor study afforded him 'the best prospect about the colledge, viz. upon the river, into the cornefields and country adjoining'.

Today's chapel was built in 1891 by Bodley and Garner: Bodley's theme of Praise is displayed in the inscriptions on the beautiful painted wooden ceiling. The glowing colours and detail in its decoration, and the opulent furnishings create an atmosphere of welcoming warmth. It is lit only by candlelight. Cromwell's servant, William Dowsing, could have spent many destructive hours here. The description of his visit to the Old Chapel on December 26th 1643 suggests a wealth of symbolic decoration at that time.

> *'We beat downe about 110 Superstitious Pictures besides Cherubims and Engravings, where none of the Fellows would put on their Hatts in all the time they were in the Chapell & we digged up the steps for 3 hours and brake down 10 or 12 Apostles & Saints within the Hall'.*

The original medieval chapel, which was consecrated in 1451 was used as a library and lecture room when the new chapel was built. Today it houses the college's War Memorial Library.

Queens' combined sundial and moondial was created in 1642 and restored in 1968. Time of day is indicated by the gnomon's shadow over the Roman numerals. The symbols of the zodiac are shown with their associated planetary object: in 1642 only 7 planets were known. The shadow of the ball on the gnomon, between the green lines, gives the zodiac phase of the year. The compass bearing of the sun, its elevation above the Horizon, and the month are also shown. However, inaccurate restoration and variables in the Earth's orbit make this unreliable.

The history of Queens' wooden bridge is frequently misrepresented. This intricate structure has earned the popular name, the Mathematical Bridge. A myth naming Sir Isaac Newton as the designer persists, even though he died in 1727, and the bridge was constructed in 1749. Queens' did, however, consult Newton on another matter in 1677, to calculate the degree of overshadowing by proposed new buildings at St Catharine's.

Tour guides often tell that the bridge was originally an ingenious interlocking, self-supporting unit, but college members had to resort to nails and bolts when they dismantled it but could not reassemble it. The bridge was actually designed by William Etheridge (who used fixings from the outset), and built by James Essex. The bridge has been renovated twice, in 1866 and 1905.

The 'Mathematical' Bridge

Queens' distinctive red brick Gate Tower

Queens' Great Gate, built in 1448, is in a quiet, shady cul-de-sac called Queens' Lane. However, when the college entrance was built, during Cambridge's sea-trading days, this was a busy road known as Milne Street. Queens' faces St Catharine's, whose Master's Lodge was built over a much disputed 10-foot-wide strip of ground, rented from Queens'. The contention over this land began in 1676, and was only settled after 137 eristic years of quarrels over leases, when Queens' sold the land to St Catharine's in 1813. Queens' alumni feature many significant leading figures. Alexander Crummell, a leading early activist for black rights, became possibly Cambridge's first black graduate in 1853. One truly 'high-flying' alumnus is N.A.S.A. astronaut Dr Colin Michael Foale, who became the first British man in space. Today Queens' specialises in drama; the erudite actor and author, Stephen Fry, graduated here in 1981.

The college insignia is the spiked wheel of Saint Catharine, which was intended to be the instrument of her execution, but broke in answer to her prayers.

ST CATHARINE'S

The spacious three-sided court of today's St Catharine's bears no resemblance to the college that Robert Wodelark, third Provost of King's College, opened in 1473. Catharine Hall began as a small clunch-built court facing away from today's King's Parade. These original buildings fronted on to what was then known as Milne Street: a major thoroughfare while Cambridge was still a sea trading port. Today this has become a quiet, shady cul-de-sac called Queens' Lane.

Things began well for Wodelark's college, which he intended for a Master and 10 Fellows. However, when Henry VI was overthrown by Edward IV, the initial financial backing reduced significantly, and the foundation charter of 1475 made provision for a Master and three or more Fellows to study philosophy and theology.

St Catharine's struggled for over a century, derided by some as 'a sucker thrown up by the parent stem' neighbouring, as it does, King's College where its founder formerly held such great status. When the town reviewed fire precautions in 1575, it accepted just two fire buckets from poor St Catharine's, when most colleges gave four.

In 1626, however, John Gostlin of Caius bequeathed the Bull Inn. Dr John Eachard's fundraising enabled building of the west and south ranges of Main Court, by Robert Grumbold. The chapel, built in 1704 on the former site of stables owned by carrier Thomas Hobson, may also be Grumbold's work. James Essex designed the Ramsden Building in 1757: this phase of building was generously funded by Mary Ramsden who left a large part of her estate to the college.

Wodelark might be gratified that his college has produced many bishops. Other notable members include John Addenbrooke, who bequeathed funds for Cambridge's famous hospital, created in 1766. He left his medicine chest to the college, and is buried in the chapel. Edward Capell, a major authority on the works of Shakespeare, studied here, as did dramatist James Shirley, between 1615 and 1617. Nevil Maskelyne, who won the title of Wrangler (having achieved a First in the Mathematical Tripos), entered the college in 1749. He was later appointed Astronomer Royal. Recent alumni include Sir Ian McKellen, Joanne Harris and Jeremy Paxman.

St Catharine's today may smile at criticism from its early years: it has flourished to become of equal size to its 'parent stem' accepting a similar number of students to King's each year.

St Catharine's is known affectionately as 'St Cat's'

JESUS

Jesus College is approached via a narrow walled path called The Chimney, leading to an impressive gate-tower which displays the founder's statue. This tower would have had even greater impact before 1718, as the original range of buildings each side were only two storeys high. The 'woodland' setting of the ancient buildings creates an ambience distinct from that of any other college.

In 1496 the bishop of Ely, John Alcock, decided to adapt the derelict 12th-century Benedictine nunnery of St Mary and St Radegund as a new college, with an attached grammar school. This ancient convent had once been a thriving establishment, and the priory's huge church had been built on land granted in 1157 by King Malcolm of Scotland, who was also Earl of Huntingdon and Cambridge.

Alcock sought permission for a charter from Pope Alexander VI and King Henry VII to refound the nunnery as 'The College of the Blessed Virgin Mary, St John the Evangelist and the Glorious Virgin St Radegund'. However, the church already had a town altar nearby, dedicated to the name of Jesus, which had given its name to Jesus Lane, and thus the title 'Jesus College' prevailed.

John Alcock, Bishop of Ely

Left: 'The Chimney'

The college motto 'Prosperum iter facias' translates as 'May your journey be successful'.

The college grew steadily in its peaceful location. King James I remarked that his ideal would be to pray at King's, dine at Trinity, and study and sleep at Jesus. The college was staunchly Royalist, and its Master, Richard Sterne, was arrested by Oliver Cromwell, while his eager assistant Dowsing 'brake down Superstitions of Saints and Angels, 120 at the least', and destroyed all the chapel's stained glass. Sterne's great-grandson, Laurence, author of *The Life and Opinions of Tristram Shandy, Gent*, studied here in the 1730s. Wayward poet Samuel Taylor Coleridge entered in 1791. He never took his degree, but loved 'the friendly cloisters and happy grove of quiet, ever-honoured Jesus College'.

Jesus College today celebrates art: the curious natural forms of topiary yew trees in the grounds are interspersed with modern sculptures. These permanent installations are complemented by visiting works when the college hosts its biennial Sculpture in the Close exhibition. The college insignia provides numerous opportunities for artistic interpretation. It is a rebus on the founder's name, Alcock, which translates naturally into the image of a cockerel and a globe.

Above: The modern student accommodation in North Court, opened in 1965, housed Prince Edward when he entered the college in 1983

Coleridge's memorial depicts the albatross from his 'Rime of the Ancient Mariner'

A Wish: Written in Jesus Wood

Lo! through the dusky silence of the groves,
Thro' vales irriguous, and thro' green retreats,
With languid murmur creeps the placid stream
And works its secret way.
Awhile meand'ring round its native fields,
It rolls the playful wave and winds its flight:
Then downward flowing with awaken'd speed
Embosoms in the Deep!
Thus thro' its silent tenor may my Life
Smooth its meek stream by sordid wealth unclogg'd,
Alike unconscious of forensic storms,
And Glory's blood-stain'd palm!
And when dark Age shall close Life's little day,
Satiate of sport, and weary of its toils,
E'en thus may slumbrous Death my decent limbs
Compose with icy hand.

Samuel Taylor Coleridge, 1792

Left: Jesus' chapel is the oldest Cambridge college building.

Thomas Cranmer, a leading figure in the Reformation, lived in Jesus College for many years. He advised Henry VIII on the divorce of his first wife, gaining great favour, as he was then appointed as the 1st Protestant Archbishop of Canterbury. The king declared of him, 'Marry! I perceive that man hath the right sow by the ear'. Henry's trust was such that he named Cranmer as one of the Council of Regency for his son Edward VI. Cranmer composed the English Litany in 1545, and wrote the '42 Articles' defining the Church of England's faith. Most unusually, he married, and so had to relinquish his fellowship at Jesus. In 1553 he was charged with treason by Henry's Catholic daughter Mary, and burned at the stake for heresy on March 21st 1556, when he refused to recant his Protestant beliefs.

Alcock modified the church considerably. He removed the side chapels, aisles and lower end of the nave, and converted other parts to the Master's Lodge. The nuns' Refectory was replaced by a new Hall; food has been served on this site for over 800 years. The cloister path, deeply worn by countless footsteps, passes three beautiful arches dating from around 1230. These arches are remnants of the entrance to the nun's Chapter-house, exposed in 1893. Recent glazing behind the arches has revealed how the ruinous 13-century building was adapted as a Fellows' room in around 1500. Restoration of the chapel began in 1846, with a reconstructed roof, new lancet windows in the chancel and a new wooden screen, all designed by Pugin. The opulent nave and tower ceilings were designed by G.F. Bodley and William Morris. The college architecture has evolved in elegant harmony with the original buildings, culminating with the beautiful Quincentenary Library which was opened by Queen Elizabeth II in 1996.

Cranmer's memorial in the chapel

Overleaf: Jesus has one of the finest Wisterias of any Cambridge College

C

The Beaufort coat of arms includes antelope-like, mythical yales, which signify proud defence. Their horns point in opposite directions. This may derive from an ancient eastern custom of training animals' horns to grow in this manner.

CHRIST'S

Lady Margaret Beaufort had a major influence on Cambridge. She held great status as King Henry VII's mother, but led a life of religious devotion, dedicated to charitable works and prayer. Her profound faith was coupled with acute intelligence, and she was well placed to observe the shifting trends of religion and politics. Thus she chose to support educational establishments rather than religious ones, for she saw clearly that a new era of logic was set to topple the Church from absolute power. She was advised by her friend and confessor, John Fisher, who was Master of Michaelhouse, before taking charge at Queens'. Together they chose God's House, created by William Bingham in 1439, to be refounded as Christ's College in 1505. Unlike Alcock's approach at Jesus College, this was a 'merger', rather than a 'takeover'. The existing Master was retained and the new society enlarged to comprise 12 fellows and up to 47 scholars: second only to King's in size.

Lady Margaret assumed an almost maternal concern for her scholars, insisting on good manners and seemly conduct. She once interceded when she 'saw the Dean call a faulty scholar to correction, to whom she said *'Lenté, lenté!'* 'Gently, gently!' as accounting it better to mitigate his punishment than to procure his pardon'. Perhaps her feminine influence may account for the college's early decor. When the Lodge was renovated by Sir Arthur Shipley between 1911 and 1920, builders discovered remnants of the earliest English wallpaper, datable to 1509.

Rather less attractive were the four mummified black rats, found at the same time in an academic nest made from shreds of a primer by Wynkyn de Worde, an edition of Horace, a 14th-century manuscript and, for light relief perhaps, four playing cards. Christ's was located perilously close to the 'King's Ditch': a filthy breeding ground for rats, where plague was a constant threat. Lady Margaret made one of her properties, Malton Farm manor house in South Cambridgeshire, available for scholars 'to resort thidder and there to tarye in tyme of siknes at Cambridge'. Over a century later, plague persisted: Dr Mead recorded on April 24th 1630:

> *'Our University is in a manner wholly dissolved: all meetings and Exersises ceasing. In many Colledges almost none left ... We have taken all our Officers we need into the Colledge and none must stirre out... Thus we live as close Prisoners, and I hope without danger.'*

Right: Christ's Master's Lodge

SOUVENT ME SOUVIENT

Christ's began a phase of regeneration in 1642, with the creation of its superb Fellows' Building. The external red brick and clunch along the street front was refaced in 1714, and James Essex was commissioned to renovate the interior of First Court between 1758 and 1770. Two further ranges of buildings were completed in 1825 and 1889. Christ's newest building is the distinctive Typewriter building, designed by Sir Denys Lasdun in 1966.

Christ's gardens form a series of immaculate courts and shady walks. A massive ancient chestnut tree in the Fellows' garden, surrounded by a snowdrops and aconites in spring, sadly succumbed to disease recently. A new garden honouring Charles Darwin was recently created, featuring plants that he would have encountered on his travels. A bronze statue of the young Darwin sits informally on the arm of a bench, surveying the scene. Close observation will reveal beside him his chief delight, a beetle!

Above: Third Court
Right: The Fellows' Building, 1642

Christ's has its own bathing pool, secluded by yew hedges and flanked by a classical summerhouse, with marble busts of Milton and philosopher Ralph Cudworth. The water comes from Hobson's Conduit: the 17th century channel created to bring clean drinking water to the town.

John Milton entered the college in 1625: his delicate appearance earned him the nickname 'The Lady of Christ's'. Another poet, the rebellious Calverley studied here in the 1850s. Philosopher and mathematician William Paley was senior wrangler in 1763. He wrote *The Evidences of Christianity*, and *Moral Philosophy* which at one time formed part of the BA Degree. It is possible to see how he may have inspired a future student at Christ's, Charles Darwin, when he says,

> *'The hinges in the wings of an earwig, and the joints of its antennae, are as highly wrought, as if the Creator had nothing else to finish. We see no signs of diminution of care by multiplicity of objects, or of distraction of thought by variety. We have no reason to fear, therefore, of our being forgotten, or overlooked, or neglected'.*

In 1608 King James I attempted to create a trading asset by cultivating mulberry trees that would support silk worms. Christ's purchased 300 trees, but the plan failed when the wrong variety, unpalatable to silkworms, was planted. This one remaining tree is named 'Milton's Mulberry': student John Milton may have been permitted to contemplate his poetry in its shade.

Charles Darwin entered the college in 1827. He originally intended to qualify as a clergyman, but admits that,

> *'Although, as we shall presently see, there were some redeeming features of my life at Cambridge, my time was sadly wasted there, and worse than wasted. From my passion for shooting and for hunting, and, when this failed, for riding across country, I got into a sporting set, including some dissipated, low-minded young men ... But no pursuit at Cambridge was followed with nearly so much eagerness or gave me so much pleasure as collecting beetles'.*

This fascination with the natural world would ironically lead him into conflict with his first intended profession when he published *The Origin of Species*: his famous theory on evolution.

Christ's today has a 'commitment to free thinking and high-achieving across many disciplines and interests'. Its alumni excel in a broad spectrum of subjects, including journalists such as BBC correspondent James Reynolds, genetic pioneer John Clark, Colin Dexter, author of the *Morse* novels, and satirist and actor Sacha Baron-Cohen (Ali G).

Right: Darwin's statue by Anthony Smith, unveiled in 2009

The ornate Beaufort insignia above the gate is surmounted by a 1662 statue of St John the Evangelist. He holds a chalice, whose contents had been poisoned by the devil. The power of the saint's prayers drove the devil out in the form of a serpent.

ST JOHN'S

Shortly after founding Christ's College, Lady Margaret Beaufort began to plan her second foundation. As mother of King Henry VII and grandmother to Henry VIII she held an unusual degree of influence for a woman of that time, and used this to pursue charitable works, guided by her advisor Bishop John Fisher. She had been considering a financial gift to Westminster Abbey, but Fisher suggested that the declining Hospital of St John, in Cambridge, had potential as an educational establishment. Lady Margaret set out instructions in her will but she would never see her second college. In 1509 she died, four days after the celebrations of her grandson Henry VIII's marriage and coronation, and the day after his birthday. It is said that she 'took her infirmity with eating of a cygnet.'

Fisher and the executors battled to obtain a charter for The College of St John the Evangelist. They finally succeeded in 1511, and the college opened in 1516. It is interesting to note the political process leading to closure of the hospital. Fifteen years earlier, Jesus College had been founded at a former nuns' priory, which was discredited to justify its dissolution. The documents denouncing St John's Hospital are virtually identical to those used against the priory, right down to the supposed number of remaining inhabitants, which was claimed to be only two. St John's evolved as a series of courts. First Court was built between 1510 and 1520. During the Civil War, Royalist prisoners were confined here.

When Second Court began in 1598, the next four years proved 'ruinous to the undertakers and not over advantageous to the College'. Mary Cavendish, Countess of Shrewsbury, could only afford £2,760 of the £3,400 she had pledged. Builder Gilbert Wigge was imprisoned for debt, and architect Ralph Symons lost his left hand during the construction. But the college continued to flourish, and by 1669, a third court was needed. This sufficed until 1826, when Rickman and Hutchinson were commissioned to design New Court.

Above: John Fisher
Right: New Court from the chapel tower
Previous page: New Court, 1831

St John's is the only college with two bridges. The Kitchen Bridge is sometimes accredited to Sir Christopher Wren. Certainly he was consulted, but his design was not used. It was built between 1696 and 1712 by Robert Grumbold, whose father built Clare's bridge 60 years earlier. The famous Bridge of Sighs was greatly admired by Queen Victoria. It was built in 1826 to complement New Court, whose elaborate gothic style has earned it the affectionate name of 'the Wedding Cake'. Sir George Gilbert Scott's controversial new chapel replaced the original one in 1869. At 50 metres, it boasts the tallest tower in Cambridge. Scott had originally intended a spire, but an alumnus pledged £5,000, to be paid over 5 years in instalments, for a tower instead. However, this scheme faltered when he was tragically killed in an accident, after only two payments, leaving the college to pay the remainder.

The Kitchen Bridge

The Bridge of Sighs

Poet William Wordsworth, who attended St John's between 1787 and 1791, describes college life in his auto-biographical poem *The Prelude.* He loved St John's natural 'Wilderness' where,

'All winter long, whenever free to choose,
Did I by night frequent the College grove
and tributary walks...'

His favourite ash tree is no more, but today he would surely appreciate the bright profusion of spring flowers which flourish here.

A gem of architectural history, the School of Pythagoras, is set within the grounds. Dated around 1200, this is the oldest domestic building in the county. It may have been one of the first teaching venues of the University, but any associations with the Greek mathematician are purely fanciful.

St John's chapel tower dominates the view from Trinity Street

The adventurous spirit of Cambridge students is exemplified by the secret, (strictly prohibited) Cambridge Night Climbers. The freshly renovated spire of the Divinity School recently tempted them to leave a sign of their conquest (right), but they have also savoured the heights of New Court's tower, where they painted a dial on the blank clock faces. Neither feat compares with the challenge of the chapel tower. With typical understatement, successful climbers describe it as 'very severe', and 'counsel enthusiasts who are more dramatically inclined to write their own epitaphs'.

In the 1770s, Cambridge University led the drive to abolish slavery, inspired by William Wilberforce, who entered St John's in 1776. This campaign lasted 19 years, backed by the Quakers and a less well-known alumnus, Thomas Clarkson, whose research for a prize-winning essay on the ethics of the slave trade moved him to speak out against it. St John's illustrious alumni also feature 9 Nobel Prize winners, 6 prime ministers and 3 archbishops. Scientists include Sir John Cockcroft, Sir Edward Appleton and Abdus Salam.

St John's Lady Margaret Boat Club (whose bright coloured rowing jackets were the original 'blazers') was the first in Cambridge, founded in 1825. In 1829 it introduced a great English tradition by challenging Oxford to a rowing contest on the Thames: the University Boat Race.

TRINITY

'To the glory of God and advantage of the realm, for the promotion of science, philosophy, liberal arts, and theology.'

This was King Henry VIII's intention in 1546, when he founded Trinity College, five weeks before his death. Trinity remains one of the largest and wealthiest colleges in the University. It has 32 Nobel Prize winners, and its diverse alumni range from Sir Isaac Newton to Alfred Lord Tennyson.

King Henry advocated 'piety, self-restraint, and knowledge, charity towards the poor, and relief of the afflicted and distressed' - ideals which may have impressed his daughter Mary, who had suffered greatly when he divorced her mother. She had little reason to honour his college, which could be seen to symbolise the age of the Reformation. And yet, as queen, she funded building of the chapel, which her sister Elizabeth saw to completion in 1564.

Henry's ambitious project commandeered a large area of the town, filling in a channel leading from the river to a wharf, and closing a lane which also led there. Two colleges, King's Hall and Michaelhouse, and at least 7 hostels were absorbed, forming a motley collection of elements for his grand new college.

Left: Founder King Henry VIII
Previous page: Trinity 'Backs'

Top: James I
Centre: Queen Elizabeth I
Below: Edward III, founder of King's Hall

Dr Thomas Nevile became Master in 1593, and set about restructuring the jumbled buildings. The pun in his motto, *Ne vile velis* (the prize should not be cheap), is most apt, for he created Nevile's Court at his own expense. Trinity's Great Court, however, is his masterpiece. Many of the original buildings were demolished, but Edward III's gate tower was preserved by moving it 20 feet back to align with the chapel.

Great Court is ingeniously asymmetrical: there are no right angles or equal sides, and the beautiful fountain, also provided by Nevile in 1602, is off-centre. The overall effect is a stunning grandeur: the vast, hushed space contrasts dramatically with the crowded street outside. The famous Great Court Run involves completing a circuit at noon within the clock's double chime. Not surprisingly, only two have achieved the 367 metres in less than 43 seconds.

Dr William Whewell (above) was Master between 1841 and 1866. He financed Trinity's extension, Whewell's Court, in 1859, and bequeathed funds for a second court, built after his death in 1866. 'Science was his forte and omniscience his foible'. Tennyson, whose statue today sits near him in the chapel, referred to him as a 'lion-like' man. Whewell's indomitable character and ferocious intellect give rise to many legends.

Whewell prided himself on having an answer for every occasion. This served him well when he undertook the duty of escorting Queen Victoria during her visit to the college. On the bridge (left) she paused, looking down into the water, which was murky with the effluent of the town. 'What are all those pieces of paper?' she enquired. 'Those, Ma'am, are notices that bathing is forbidden', came the inspired reply.

Sir Isaac Newton's statue, carved by Roubillac, was installed in the chapel in 1755. Wordsworth recalls its compelling moonlit presence:

'In the antechapel, where the statue stood
Of Newton, with his prism and silent face;
The marble index of a mind forever
Voyaging through strange seas of
thought alone.'

Sir Isaac Newton resided at Trinity between 1661 and 1696. Today, an apple tree stands before his rooms beside the Great Gate - a descendant of the original *Flower of Kent* whose falling fruit inspired Newton to the theory of gravity. He is described as a mild, modest man, preoccupied with abstract thoughts. This once led to disastrous results, when he accidentally overturned a candle, and set fire to research twenty years in the making. Newton determined the speed of sound under the cloisters on the North side of Nevile's court, by tapping his foot and timing the echo.

Trinity's library was designed, free of charge, by Sir Christopher Wren. The library's interior was also designed by Wren, who provided revolving book rests, and bookshelves arranged to create private study areas. There are around 90,000 books. Precious manuscripts include Milton's first sketch for *Paradise Lost*, and an 8th century copy of St Paul's Epistles. There is also A.A. Milne's original manuscript of *Winnie the Pooh*: both Milne and his son, Christopher Robin, studied at Trinity. The library is adorned with limewood carvings of fruit and flowers, and many marble sculptures. The finest and most controversial statue is Trinity student Lord Byron, which was twice offered to Westminster Abbey but rejected because of his immoral reputation.

Above: The windows of Newton's rooms
Right: The Wren Library
Overleaf: Trinity's bridge & avenue in spring

EMMANUEL

Queen Elizabeth I: 'I hear, Sir Walter, that you have erected a Puritan foundation'.
Sir Walter Mildmay: 'No, Madam, far be it from me to countenance anything contrary to your established laws; but I have set an acorn, which, when it becomes an oak, God alone knows what will be the fruit thereof.

Sir Walter's acorn, set in 1584, would produce free-thinking 'fruit' that would spread across the world. His college grew on the site of a Dominican friars' monastery, established early in the 13th century. As the name Emmanuel suggests, Christianity was the college's primary focus. Moreover, Mildmay intended to send the Gospel far afield, stating that, 'We would not have any Fellow suppose that we have given him in this College a perpetual abode'.

The devout Mildmay discouraged feasting, playing and talking, and ordered frequent chapel attendances, nightly prayers and extra Sunday lectures on the Christian faith. The first Master, Laurence Chaderton could hold a congregation spellbound for two hours, only to be implored 'For God's sake, sir, go on!'. He lived to be over 100: a record among Cambridge and Oxford Heads of Houses. In the 1630s the college's religious fervour inspired 35 Emmanuel men to take the Gospel to America. Among them was John Harvard, who bequeathed his library and half his estate to America's first university. Sir Walter's reassurance to the Queen may have been eloquently neutral, but the north-south orientation of Emmanuel's new chapel symbolised his rejection of Catholic ideals, for chapels traditionally faced east-west. This won Cromwell's approval during the 1640s, when he imposed eight Emmanuel members as masters of Royalist colleges in Cambridge.

The chapel window depicting Harvard & Chaderton

Sir Christopher Wren's design for the chapel was instigated by William Sancroft in 1666, and is once more aligned east-west to remove 'the former singularity which rendered us heretofore so unhappily remarkable'. Its chandelier dates from 1732, and the altar piece by Jacopo Amigoni was presented in 1734. The exceptional windows commemorate Cambridge figures including Harvard and Chaderton.

Left: Emmanuel's Chapel by Sir Christopher Wren

'The Jester' by Wendy Taylor

Henry VIII dissolved the friary in 1538 but spared the buildings. When Ralph Symons undertook their renovation, his main change was to create a north-south facing chapel. Sir Walter's 'nursery of Puritanism' flourished until the Royalist Restoration in 1660, and Sir Christopher Wren's new chapel symbolised this new era in its re-orientation of east-west. Built in 1677, it stands as a separate building, with its roof linked to the long gallery which runs above the cloisters. The Founder's Range was rebuilt in 1719. James Burrough was asked to redesign the St Andrew's Street side of the college in 1752, but when he died 12 years later, James Essex completed the project.

Sir Walter would have regarded 18th century Emmanuel in dismay. Between 1775 and 1797 the Master was 'Rare Richard Farmer': a genial host to all 'who loved pipes and tobacco and cheerful conversation'. He adored the theatre. Each year at Sturbridge Fair he and his 'Shakespeare Gang' of friends would watch every play, enthusiastically applauding all. More decadent still, the Combination Room kept a Wager Book, where the stakes were usually wine! During the French Revolution the book records a successful wager that Marat would be murdered before the end of the Lent Term but an optimistic bet in 1794, that the War would be over in two years, was lost.

The college was originally entered from Emmanuel Street, but this gate was closed following renovation of the St Andrew's Street side. This rearrangement meant that visitors would now appreciate Wren's magnificent architecture on entering the college rather than Emmanuel's lovely grounds, which have become a verdant jewel waiting to be discovered. The dignified confines of Front Court contrast dramatically with these vast, informal gardens, which are exceptionally beautiful in spring, when they are bright with daffodils, and blossom enhances the reflections in Paddock's pond. Many ducks and moorhens inhabit this pool, which once supplied the Dominican monks with fish. It was here that the eminent scientist Thomas Young, who also worked to decipher the Rosetta Stone, was said to have been inspired to his wave-theory of light by the ripples on the water.

Emmanuel receives water from Hobson's conduit, which runs in a stream through the grounds and fills the 300 year-old Fellows' swimming pool. Before the days of chemical water treatment, lines were painted on the bottom of this pool to guide underwater swimmers through the algae-rich water. The Fellows' garden has many beautiful trees, including a magnificent 200 year-old Oriental Plane.

The college built North Court in 1913, full of optimism as student numbers increased. But the next year WW1 decimated admissions, and North Court served the War Office by accommodating officers on training courses. After the war, the college flourished again with three Nobel Prize winners: Frederick Gowland Hopkins in 1929, for his discovery of vitamins, and the prize for Chemistry awarded jointly to George Porter and Ronald George Wreyford Norrish in 1967.

Right: Paddock's Pond

SIDNEY SUSSEX

This college, tucked discreetly behind a high wall in Sidney Street, was founded in 1596: the bequest of Frances, Countess of Sussex, daughter of Sir William Sidney. It was formerly a Franciscan friary, which settled on this site in the 1260s but was dissolved, of course, by Henry VIII in 1538. The University had been eager to acquire it immediately, arguing that it was 'not only a grace and ornament to the University, but (it) presents great conveniences for holding congregations and transacting all kinds of University business'. However, in 1546 they were disappointed when it was given to Trinity College who promptly dismantled the friary stonework to help construct this, King Henry VIII's new project. In 1594 Queen Elizabeth I intervened, granting a licence for the College's foundation, and Trinity conveyed the site to Sidney Sussex the following year.

Lady Frances had bequeathed funds for the project, but even in the 16th century it was a scanty provision. The writer Thomas Fuller remarked, 'Alas! What is five thousand pounds to buy the site, build and endow a College therewith?' Nevertheless the executors competently nurtured the college in its infancy, creating, as Lady Frances wished, 'a godlie monument for the mainteynance of good learninge'.

By 1594, Trinity College had picked the bones of the monastery almost clean, leaving only one building unscathed. On the strength of his work at Emmanuel, Ralph Symons was chosen to design this new college and the first stone was laid on May 20th 1595. A three-sided court was complete by 1598, with an ornate gatehouse central in the enclosing wall on the southern side. This layout emulated that of Gonville and Caius College, which aimed to encourage air circulation and reduce risk of plague.

Magnificent Wisteria beside Sidney Street

Jeffrey Wyatt was chosen to update the college between 1821 and 1832. His additions conceal Ralph Symons' original red brick walls beneath distinctive gables and Roman cement facing. Wyatt's style was much favoured by George IV, who commissioned him for improvements to Windsor Castle and knighted him Sir Jeffrey Wyattville.

Sidney Sussex was the second puritan foundation in Cambridge, which made it a natural choice for Oliver Cromwell, who, at the age of 17, entered the college on April 23rd 1616. However, only one year later, when his father died, Cromwell had to leave to support his family. It seems there was no time for him to develop any affection for his college. When it sent silver to the king during the Civil War, Cromwell cruelly punished its elderly Master, Samuel Ward. In 1643, along with Masters of other colleges, he was taken prisoner, 'on an exceedingly cold night till near one in the morning, without any accommodation for food, firing or lodging; and to complete the outrage, it was done on Good Friday, whence it may be supposed that they went with empty stomachs'. Poor Samuel Ward died shortly afterwards. The college bitterly recorded beside Cromwell's name in its admission book:

> *'This was that great impostor, that most accursed butcher, who when the most pious King Charles had been disposed of by foul murder, usurped the throne itself, and for the space of almost five years, under the name of Protector, tormented the three kingdoms with unrestrained tyranny'.*

Cromwell died of malaria on September 3rd, 1658, but the Restored Royalists exhumed his body, hanged and beheaded him. His head was displayed on a pole in London for 25 years, until a storm dislodged it. Three obscure centuries later, it was returned to Sidney Sussex, and in 1960 the college laid their persecutor and 'prodigal son' to rest at last, in a secret place in the chapel. In 1766 the college received Cromwell's pastel portrait by the workshop of Sir Peter Lely, who he famously instructed, 'not flatter me at all, but remark all these roughnesses, pimples, warts, and everything as you see me, otherwise I never will pay a farthing for it'.

Exceptional woodcarving in the chapel depicts the birds beloved by St Francis

Aconites in Cloister Court

In the shady peace of the cloisters, the noise of shoppers passing just the other side of the college wall fades to insignificance. Sidney Sussex's carefully tended grounds are a green sanctuary which maintains the air of a country garden; occasional sculptures set within the grounds provide additional interest. The springtime masses of anemones, daffodils, snowdrops and aconites create carpets of colour beneath the stately trees. Even the austerity of the courtyards is softened by a variety of climbing plants. In May the masses of purple wisteria flowers along the walls are especially impressive.

Sidney Sussex's achievements have flourished as quietly as the flowers in its gardens. Although the college experienced a lull in the early 1800s, (apparently at one point it had but a single undergraduate), it has produced many notable writers and mathematicians. Maths Fellow Gordon Welchman, John Herivel and Leslie Yoxall were key figures in breaking the Enigma code during WW2. Today Sidney Sussex is fourth in Cambridge's college league of Nobel prize winners, with five to its name. These prizes are mainly for science, but the college also excels in the arts, mathematics, humanities and law.

DOWNING

Sir George Downing died in 1749, leaving a substantial fortune with which he intended to found a college if none of his four cousins produced heirs. But he was to be frustrated in death, as he had been in life. Poor Sir George was three when his mother died, and he was sent to live with his aunt and uncle, who arranged his marriage to their 13 year-old daughter when he was aged 15. Against his wishes, she went to serve as lady-in-waiting to Queen Anne, and he obtained legal permission for them to live apart while still married. The embittered Sir George was once attacked with a hammer by a tenant because he 'paid nobody, and was so ill a landlord and paymaster with so great an estate'. He died childless. When his last cousin likewise passed away in 1764, the University should have received his bequest, but Lady Downing contested this until her death in 1778. Litigation continued between the University and her heirs, further draining the family estate until 1802 .

A charter for the college was finally obtained in 1800, but it took some time for plans to take shape. James Essex had offered designs in 1771, and James Wyatt suggested four façades arranged along the Backs. Parker's Piece and Castle Hill were also considered as potential sites. Finally, a vast stretch of land between St Andrew's Street and Pembroke was purchased, and in 1806 William Wilkins produced the designs as King George III wished, in a style 'definitely not Gothic'. Wilkins' work here is in a Greek classical style - a total departure from his other Cambridge buildings. Downing's west wing was finished by 1820, but the east side lay part-built until E.M. Barry completed it in 1875. To cover financial difficulties, a substantial northern section of the grounds was gradually sold to the University between 1895 and 1905. The laboratories built there today are referred to as the Downing Site.

Left: Downing's grounds are spectacular in Spring

The creation of the College chapel was also protracted. Downing's first Professor of Medicine, eminent scientist Sir Busick Harwood, died in 1814, and wished to be buried on the intended site of the chapel. Due to adverse weather conditions at the time, Sir Busick's coffin was interred in a temporary situation, but the unfortunate gentleman rested there in an unmarked grave for 173 years. Downing's chapel was finally built in 1953 in a different location on the opposite side of the quadrangle and a memorial plaque now marks Sir Busick's resting place.

As the millennium approached, Downing engaged Quinlan Terry to design a series of developments. These were funded by generous benefactors, especially the Howard family, who financed buildings in 1985 and 1994, providing additional student accommodation and conference facilities. A new student bar, the Butterfield Building, opened in 1989: this is now a daytime café which is open to the public. In 2010 they also funded the new Howard Theatre, which completed Howard Court. Quinlan's classical style continues the original architectural theme, and his theatre is inspired by William Wilkins' Theatre Royal in Bury St Edmunds. If the intended quadrangle of Downing's buildings were completed on the south side, its area would trump Trinity College's Great Court. There is an urban myth that Trinity pays Downing an annual sum never to enclose the area, which would rob them of their claim to the largest court in Cambridge or Oxford. Downing's alumni excel in many areas, but the most familiar names are comedian John Cleese and artist Quentin Blake.

In 1987 J.W.C Maitland Robinson donated funds for Downing's first ever purpose-built library (left). Quinlan Terry was once again commissioned as designer. The library's distinctive octagonal tower is inspired by the Tower of Winds: a 2,000 year-old marble tower in Athens which features a wind vane, sundials and a water clock.

Left: The Maitland Library
Right: Diligent care of Downing's extensive lawns!

DON PASQUALE
M&S FOODHALL
CHORIZO GRILL
£5 a Roll
TRY OUR DELICIOUS
ADDITIVE & GLUTEN
FREE SPANISH
CHORIZO!
FOR
TODAY

THE MARKET

Cambridge has been an important trade centre since Roman times – sea horses and ships on its crest illustrate that, along with many fenland towns, it was once a sea port. Today's market square once formed an L-shape around a block of houses which was destroyed by the Great Fire of 1849. This important public space has been centre-stage for many Cambridge dramas, from the medieval Peasants' Revolt, when books looted from the colleges were burned here, to costly destruction by male undergraduates, rioting against women's rights in the 1870s. On 6th February 1556, during Mary Tudor's vengeful restoration of Catholicism, fanatical townsfolk exhumed and 'crated' the bodies of two despised Protestant reformers, Paul Fagius and Martin Bucer. These were paraded to the market by earth-smeared priests and crowds with flaming torches.

> *'a great poste was set faste in the ground to bynde the carcases to … When they came thyther, the chestes were set up on end, wyth ye dead bodyes in them, and fastened on both sides wyth stakes, and bound to the poste with a long yron chayne as if they had bene alive. Fyre being forthwith put to, as soone as it began to flame rounde aboute, a great sorte of bookes that were condemned wyth them, were caste into the same'.*

The market is dominated by Great St Mary's, the University's own church. This landmark is the starting point for milestones on the road to London, which were installed in 1730 for Trinity Hall's lawyers, who often commuted to the capital. The church's chimes, by Trinity Hall's Dr Jowett, have become famous worldwide as the sound of Big Ben at Westminster.

Left: Cambridge Market
Above: The Duke & Duchess' first Cambridge visit

St Bene't's Church is the oldest building in Cambridge, with a tower built in 1025. Inside are a Saxon archway and beautiful painted woodwork. Its bells were the first to ring out an organised peal, with a system devised in the 1670s by Fabian Stedman. St Bene't's keeps a bible donated by Thomas Hobson, and also an ancient fire hook for pulling burning thatch from houses. Corpus Christi used this church until their own chapel was built in 1579.

CHURCHES

The Church of the Holy Sepulchre, commonly known as the Round Church, dates from 1130 and is the second oldest building in Cambridge. Its shape emulates the original in Jerusalem. One of only four round churches in the country, it stands as an ancient island in a sea of change. The building has been altered many times, especially in the 1840s, when Norman-style windows and doors were installed by the over-zealous Cambridge Camden Society. Pictures from the 15th century show a polygonal, not a conical tower. Inside, however, the circular nave with its carved stone faces on the pillars remains unchanged. The newest window, which replaces one bomb-damaged during the course of World War 2, depicts Christ crucified on the living Tree of Life, symbolising new beginnings.

Cambridge churches are often older than they appear. St Edward King and Martyr, in St Edward's Passage, is described as 'the cradle of the Reformation'. The religious reformer and Clare Fellow, Hugh Latimer, gave many inspiring sermons here during the 1500s. The tower of St Botolph's, at the end of King's Parade features four curious statues of the evangelists. Medieval travellers would stop to pray here as they passed the town's defensive gates.

When Jesus referred to 'two or three gathered together', he could have had St Peter's Church on Castle Hill in mind. Only 30 feet long, it is Cambridge's smallest church. St Peter's has two Saxon arches, and a remarkable stone font with four carved mermen. Fragments of Roman tiles embedded in the walls support the theory that a Roman temple once stood here. Although no longer actively used, its history of devotion makes this place arguably 'one of the holiest places in the city'. In dramatic contrast, with a spire 216 feet high, the ornate Roman Catholic Church of Our Lady and the English Martyrs, towers over the junction of Hills Road and Lensfield Road. It was completed in 1890, financed by the renowned ballet dancer Mrs Lyne-Stephens.

Opposite St John's College once stood All Saints in the Jewry, which projected into the street at right angles, with an arched walkway beneath its tower. This church eventually became such an obstruction to traffic that a new All Saints was built in Jesus Lane. On 24th May 1865, all the materials of the ancient church, except for the bells and stone floor, were auctioned off.

Right: The Round Church

SAINT JOHNS STREET
HARDYS SWEETSHOP

AROUND TOWN

Cambridge city centre owes its unique layout to the ancient stone buildings of the University. Along Trinity Lane history is captured in a patchwork of brick and stone, while the fortress-like gates of the colleges are a reminder of violent times when 'town and gown' conflicts were regular occurrences. Satirical verse celebrates a pitched battle in Rose Crescent in 1846,

Fitz-Wiggins floored fierce Freestone, Tom Noddy levelled Hobbs,
And cheerful Merrypebbles blackened both the eyes of Dobbs;
And the aggravated townsmen stand all aghast to see
On the flags the unconscious Peelers, in the Pass the dauntless Three.
And on the leaguered Crescent, was none would brave attack;
But those behind cried 'Forward!' And those in front cried 'Back!'

Medieval Magdalene Street

The stone walls of Garret Hostel Lane were worn away by the flanks of cattle from bygone times, as they headed for pastures by the river. Cobblestoned Green Street takes its optimistic name from grim times. This street became overgrown when its plague-stricken inhabitants were walled in, as a desperate attempt to limit the disease. Petty Cury has witnessed more light-hearted times, when students enjoyed the unlikely sport of catching ladies at midday and turning them upside down!

While stone buildings have endured, many lesser structures have been swept away. Petty Cury was once a picturesque alley of medieval timber framed shops. In Bridge Street, the remaining ancient buildings owe their survival to lack of funds for renovation in the 1960s. Across the bridge, in Magdalene street, things are very much as Samuel Pepys would have seen them in the 1660s, including one of his favourite haunts during sermon time, the Pickerel public house.

Left: Ancient stonework in Trinity Lane

Portugal Place

An essential luxury for senior University members has always been their after-dinner drink of port. Large quantities were imported (from Portugal, of course), and stored in warehouses near Quayside, giving rise to the name Portugal Place. Today, you can find historic Cambridge encapsulated in this quiet terraced street. The elegant town houses in Malcolm Street, which were originally upmarket dwellings, are now demoted to offices or student accommodation, while the servants' homes of New Square and Newnham have become fashionable bijou residences.

Right: Original gas lamp in Fair Street

Away from the centre, many sleepy lanes reveal history in their names and buildings. Some streets are lit by an original gas lamp, and cobblestones occasionally peep through scanty tarmac. Paradise Street and Adam and Eve Street both take their name from a former market garden nicknamed the Garden of Eden. Near Little St Mary's church is a building with an iron railing fixed outside the top corner window. In 1756 a Peterhouse scholar, the poet Thomas Gray, lodged here. He was terrified that the rowdy students downstairs would set the place on fire, and asked the college to install this railing so that he could escape down a rope ladder if necessary. Pranksters raised a false fire alarm and put a bath of cold water below his window, hoping he would fall in. The Rev. John Sharp, of Peterhouse reported, unsympathetically,

> *'A delicate white nightcap is said to have appeared at the window, but, finding the mistake, retired again to the couch. The young fellows, had he descended, were determined, they said, to have whipped the butterfly up again'.*

Gray promptly sought a happier life at nearby Pembroke College.

Hobson died on New Year's Day, 1631, aged 86, while the town was quarantined due to plague and his normal delivery service to London had been suspended. Milton's satirical verse summed up the irony of his passing:

'Rest that gives all men life, gave him his death,
And too much breathing put him out of breath,
Nor were it contradiction to affirm
Too long vacation hastened on his term'

HOBSON'S CONDUIT

The roadside runnels that occasionally trap unwary motorists along Trumpington Street were created 400 years ago. Although named Hobson's Conduit, this project was first suggested by Andrew Perne, of Peterhouse, in 1574. Stephen Perse, of Caius College, finished the job in 1614, at last bringing fresh water to the plague-ridden town from Nine Wells, near the Gog Magog hills south of Cambridge. Channels lead to the town centre via Trumpington Street and underground along St Andrew's Street. For 235 years, the conduit supplied the fountain in the market square, as well as Christ's College swimming pool and Emmanuel's ponds. When the 'Great Fire' of Cambridge destroyed the market in 1849, a new fountain was built, and the original one moved to the corner of Lensfield Road.

Thomas Hobson was a key sponsor of the project. He kept stables in what is now part of the grounds of St Catharine's College; one of the water channels ran conveniently past it. The saying, 'Hobson's choice, that or none', originated here. His University customers were notorious for riding hard, and Hobson insisted that they 'take the horse by the stable door', meaning the horse that had rested longest.

Hobson's Conduit in Trumpington Street

JUDGE BUSINESS SCHOOL

This was formerly Addenbrookes Hospital, whose first buildings were bequeathed in 1766 by eminent physician, Dr John Addenbrooke. He is described as 'a tall thin man skilled in necromancy': his nurse during his final days said he predicted the time of his own death to within five minutes. In 1866 Sir Matthew Digby Wyatt remodelled the original buildings to the style of today. By 1948 the hospital needed to expand. A new development along Hills Road began, where patients were first treated in 1961, but for 23 years the old hospital also remained in use. It closed in 1984, and stood empty for eight years, escaping demolition thanks to its listed building status.

The new Business School, opened in 1995 by Queen Elizabeth II, was financed by Sir Paul and Lady Judge, with the Monument Trust. Architect John Outram converted the interior into an environment that supports the School's ideals of openness and collaboration, using vibrant colours, strong geometric forms, 'floating' staircases and open balconies. A £34 million expansion project is currently underway.

PECK
SON
SPENSING
CHEMISTS
Est 1851

FITZWILLIAM MUSEUM

Richard, seventh Viscount Fitzwilliam, studied at Trinity Hall. He was a keen collector of art, and in 1816 he bequeathed his library, collection of paintings, and £100,000 to the University to build a place worthy of housing them. The collection has grown steadily, and today The Fitzwilliam Museum is home to half a million treasures of national and international significance.

The museum has a substantial collection from Egypt, including the granite head of a Pharaoh from the Middle Kingdom, and a sarcophagus lid of Rameses III. The Roman and Greek artefacts are of special interest. There are also exhibits of coins, ceramics, and textiles, not to mention an impressive selection of armour and weapons, guaranteed to delight any young would-be warrior.

The extensive collection of ancient and modern manuscripts includes John Keats' *Ode to a Nightingale*. It also holds an important series of Handel manuscripts, and autographed compositions by Purcell, Bach and Mozart. The range of art encompasses works from Rembrandt and Rubens to Picasso and Barbara Hepworth, along with numerous old master drawings, watercolours and engravings. The collection is constantly evolving, and it regularly hosts additional visiting collections. The building itself deserves as much attention as its contents. Its Corinthian façade is an imposing feature of Trumpington Street, guarded by four huge stone lions. The foundation stone was laid in 1837, but the first architect, George Basevi, tragically fell to his death from scaffolding at Ely Cathedral before the museum's completion. The work was continued by C.R. Cockerell, who designed the impressive bronze doors, and E.M. Barry completed the entrance hall in 1875. The Fitzwilliam is described today as 'One of the greatest art collections of the nation and a monument of the first importance'.

THE MITRE
FOUNDED IN 1754
GREENE KING
THE BARON OF BEEF
COTE

THE UNIVERSITY

Cambridge University first dates back to 1209, when scholars fleeing from riots in Oxford took refuge here. The early colleges were founded by religious orders or high-born wealthy and charitable individuals, often women. The ravages of the Black Death in medieval times gave rise to more colleges, quickly established to train new priests, to replace the great number of clergy wiped out by the plague. Scholars usually began at the University around age 14, often with only a little knowledge of Latin, and their first task was to master this language. They would then take the Trivium, a threefold course in grammar, logic & rhetoric. Further studies in the Quadrivium: arithmetic, geometry, music & astronomy, qualified the student to become a lecturer and to use the title Master of Arts. Up until around 1772 examinations were oral, not written. Today's examination term, *Tripos*, originates from the three-legged stool where the candidate sat during these disputations.

The range of subjects studied slowly expanded to incorporate law & medicine, but being a confirmed member of the Church remained a prerequisite for a degree until 1871. College Fellows, elected to undertake specialist teaching or research, could not marry unless they gave up their fellowship. The first three colleges for women were introduced between 1869-1885, although women could not hold official degrees until 1947. It would then be a further 25 years until the other colleges began to accept female students. The University today comprises 31 colleges, engaged at the forefront of global intellectual advancement. The life of a Cambridge student is often perceived by outsiders as one of decadent indulgence, but the privileges of studying at Cambridge come at the price of a heavy workload. It is a fine thing to march proudly at the head of the procession on Graduation Day, to receive a First, but others further down the line may have suffered. This has ever been the case. The eminent philosopher William Paley, himself of Christ's College, commented in 1797:

> *'You may do anything with young men by encouragement, by prizes, honours and distinctions; see what is done at Cambridge. But there the stimulus is too strong; two or three heads are cracked by it every year … some of them go mad, others are reduced to such a state of debility, both of the mind and body, that they are unfit for anything during the rest of their lives.'*

When students matriculate (enrol with a college), they are assigned a tutor who oversees academic progress and welfare, whilst their daily coming and goings are watched over by vigilant Porters, who are no mere luggage bearers. These official gate-keepers have an impressive knowledge of staff & students. In extreme cases of misconduct a student may be *sent down* i.e. expelled; not to be confused with *going down* from college during holiday time. At one time the disgraced undergraduate's friends would escort his last journey to the station in a mock funeral procession.

Left: Magdalene's Master, Dr Rowan Williams leads his graduands to Senate House

When graduates emerge triumphantly into Senate House Passage with their certificates they are met and congratulated by proud lecturers and tutors.

The narrow space between Caius College and Senate House roof (revealed in the skyline above) provides a famous challenge for some of Cambridge's more adventurous 'high-flying' students, who launch themselves across the gap.

THE CONGREGATIONS

Graduation days see the Masters of the colleges leading their graduands to the Congregations at Senate House, for the ceremony in which they will become fully-fledged graduates. In the narrow streets, crowds of townsfolk and tourists part like the waters of the Red Sea as the procession passes, closing in once more when it has gone by, with scarcely a comment. It is a quiet, curious illustration of the timeless parallel existences of 'Town and Gown'. The procession assembles in the street outside Senate House prior to the ceremony. Once inside, the Praelector, the Fellow responsible for the college's undergraduates, presents the graduands to their Master, four at a time. Each holds one of his fingers while he recites the Latin words admitting them to their degree. They kneel in turn before him while this is granted. On receiving their certificate they depart out into the daylight as graduates, to commence celebrations.

A bewildering 30 variations of gowns may be seen. Subtle differences in sleeve design indicate the college, whilst hood colour denotes the degree. Soft, tasselled 'beefeater' bonnets and red gowns are reserved for doctorates (hence Scarlet Days – religious festivals and degree days, when doctors of the university are required to wear full academic dress). Until 1943 the square mortar board hat was compulsory uniform for students. From its basic original purpose of keeping scholars warm in draughty medieval colleges, the most high ranking academic gowns have been elevated to a work of art. The Chancellor's gold lace trimmed black silk gown alone is worth £35,000. The two main Cambridge tailors are Ede & Ravenscroft, established in 1689, and Ryder & Amies, which has traded under the management of one family for over 120 years.

The ancient titles for University officials are also intriguing. The Orator, an office that has existed since 1522, writes formal University letters, and presents honorary degree recipients to the Chancellor. Proctors traditionally oversaw college discipline, but their duties are now largely ceremonial. Esquire Bedells carry impressive silver maces, presented by the Duke of Buckingham in 1626. Bulldogs carry halberds instead: they originally enforced order among the students, and patrolled the streets in pairs: one chosen for speed, the other for stamina in the chase.

Above: The Duke of Edinburgh's final ceremony as Chancellor
Right: Graduands processing along King's Parade

The Senate House and Old Schools (to the left)

THE SENATE HOUSE

Degree results are shown on the display boards outside Senate House

This stately building, designed by James Essex, has been the venue for University Congregations since 1730. Before then, degrees were conferred at Great St Mary's. The Senate House sits at right angles to the 15th century Old Schools whose complementary façade was added in 1755 by Stephen Wright. These were the original lecture rooms of the University and housed the main University library until 1934. During the 1800s, a protracted debate on how to accommodate the ever-expanding library and provide adequate lecture facilities brought both buildings under threat of demolition. Years of dispute ended when lack of funds decided the matter.

The expanse of lawn in front of Senate House provides a luxurious sense of space amid Cambridge's narrow streets, emphasising the location's significance. Central to the scene stands a huge vase, known as the Warwick vase. This is a replica of a Roman marble urn found in marshy ground near Hadrian's villa at Tivoli. The original is kept at the Burrell Collection in Glasgow. Graduation days are the only times of the year the hallowed grass may be walked upon. On these occasions the customary stillness is replaced by colourful crowds of people. New graduates in immaculate black gowns mingle with family members in their finery to celebrate this important rite of passage.

10

GIRTON

Girton, the first residential college for women, was initially based at Benslow House in Hitchin. It opened on 16th October, 1869 thanks to the efforts of Emily Davies, supported by Lady Stanley of Alderley and Madame Barbara Bodichon who donated generous funds. Emily Davies had achieved several victories for girls' education during the 1860s, but opposed the University's simplified Examinations for Women, asserting that women should take the same Honours degree as Cambridge's male students. Girton's first five students worked at degree level, but University rules at that time excluded them from actually claiming the titles for their achievement.

Benslow House soon proved too small. With propriety in mind today's site, on the northern edge of Cambridge city centre, was selected. The original buildings, designed by Alfred Waterhouse, opened in 1873, set amidst playing fields, woodland, and a beautiful orchard. The college's outstanding library was built in 1884. Girton needed an excellent resource because its students could not access the University libraries, and early donors of books include George Eliot and Tennyson. Girton reveals its specialism in the arts with many paintings and sculptures on display throughout the College, and also has a rich musical tradition.

Girton gained full college status in 1948, when it awarded the first woman's Honorary Degree to Queen Elizabeth, consort to King George VI. In 1976, Girton became one of the first coeducational colleges, and today is proud of its dedication to student equality.

NEWNHAM

In 1871, Newnham College began life in a small house in Regent Street, Cambridge, with five students, a Principal and a small band of ardent well-wishers. It had no recognition, no status, no money and certainly no official encouragement. Lectures for women had begun in 1870 but Millicent Garrett Fawcett, who later became a celebrated campaigner for women's suffrage, urged the philosopher Henry Sidgwick to rent the Regent Street property for the young women to live in, albeit at the risk of his own reputation. He, in turn, persuaded Anne Jemima Clough, who had previously run her own school in the Lake District, to take charge of this house.

Many of the young ladies had no access to formal secondary schooling, and so Newnham's founders allowed them to study at a level appropriate to their individual attainments and abilities. Demand steadily increased and Newnham Hall opened its doors in 1875, set in the spacious and beautiful grounds where it remains today. The early senior College members included some passionate horticulturists. They created the college's delightful gardens, secluded by the buildings, which are often referred to today as one of Cambridge's hidden secrets.

The University as an institution had, at first, taken no notice of Newnham's students, who had to negotiate to sit their examinations with each examiner individually. However, in 1881, a general permission was agreed. In 1890 the University could not fail to notice Philippa Fawcett, daughter of Millicent, when she was ranked above the Senior Wrangler: i.e. top in the Mathematical Tripos, which was seen by many as the 'blue riband' in Cambridge examinations. The impact that Newnham was having on transforming women's lives was now becoming difficult to ignore. Women were permitted to sit exams, and received certificates from their Colleges, but the next step was to try to secure the titles of their degrees. A first attempt was rebuffed in 1887, and the second effort in 1897 went down to even more spectacular defeat. In 1948, women were finally admitted to full membership of Cambridge, the last University in the UK to do so, but the University authorities retained powers to limit the number of women until 1981.

Today Newnham, in the heart of Cambridge, is a lively, stimulating college run by women, for women. Its mission is to provide its 700 exceptional students with an inspiring education, which enables them to embrace challenges, aspire, achieve and lead.

Newnham women have played a significant part in history. In WW2, Lucia Windsor and Dorothy Garrod played vital roles in RAF reconnaissance and mapping. Camilla Wedgwood went behind Japanese enemy lines in Papua New Guinea to advise the tribes she had previously worked with on assisting advancing Australian forces.

Rosalind Franklin's work on DNA paved the way for Crick and Watson's famous discovery of its double helix structure. The exceptional chemist Dorothy Hodgkin was the first British woman to receive a Nobel Prize, in 1964.

Notable recent alumnae include Emma Thompson, Clare Balding, Anna Watkins, Ali Smith, Germaine Greer and Mary Beard.

Selwyn Chapel

SELWYN

Selwyn College was founded in 1882 with 28 students 'willing to live economically with a College wherein sober living and high culture of the mind may be combined with Christian training, based upon the principles of the Church of England'. It was named after Bishop George Augustus Selwyn, who became the first Bishop of New Zealand, from 1841-1868, and then Bishop of Lichfield.

At first, some argued that the site was too far out of town. But the original farmland setting has since been developed and the college today is close to the geographical heart of the University, next to the Sidgwick site. Selwyn remains true to its first egalitarian principles, as a broadly-based College with a higher-than-average percentage of students from state schools.

Selwyn's first set of buildings were all designed by Sir Arthur Blomfield. His Tudor Gothic chapel had to be reduced by several feet to save money.

The chapel forms a striking backdrop to the tranquil gardens, where wide grassy paths wind between herbaceous borders and stately trees, leading to a picturesque pond.

During WW2, Selwyn's spacious courtyards were cultivated to support the war effort!

Life was frugal for all at first. The college was still a building site, and the chapel was built as a priority over the dining hall. Although water closets were installed in 1913, tin baths were needed until 1927. Peterhouse received electricity in 1884, but Selwyn had to wait until 1923. The college's eccentric debating society disputed subjects ranging from 'further operations in the matter of the Channel Tunnel' to a motion that 'lectures are a farce'. Selwyn today has a strong reputation in music, but the sober repertoire of early days failed to please: the Master complained of audiences who 'pelt the performers and interpolate choruses'.

The library was built in 1929 as a memorial to members lost in WW1. During WW2 the porters' lodge became an air raid warden's post, with the town's warning siren on the tower. In 1958 Selwyn at last dispelled its early image as a training ground for the clergy by gaining full college status, and in 1976 it became one of Cambridge's first co-educational colleges. In the new millennium, Chris and Ann Dobson funded the elegant Ann's Court. Selwyn's alumni include John Gummer, Clive Anderson, and novelist Robert Harris. The physician and Olympic rowing gold medallist William Laurie also studied here, as did his son, Hugh Laurie.

The elegant new cloisters of Ann's Court

HUGHES HALL

Hughes Hall is the oldest of Cambridge's six graduate colleges, and also admits undergraduate students over the age of 21. It began in 1885 as the Cambridge Training College for Women Teachers, and occupies the same pleasant site on the edge of the city centre, where it overlooks the University's famous cricket ground, Fenners (founded in 1820). The college's first building, built by W.C. Fawcett, is now a listed historic building.

By 1899 the College had already trained over 500 women, and had 60 residential students. The University allowed women to become full members in 1948, and the following year the College changed its name to Hughes Hall in honour of the first Principal, Elizabeth Phillips Hughes. During the 1970s it was the first all-women college to admit male students, and it became a full College of the University in 2006. Hughes Hall has students across a wide range of disciplines and is particularly strong in Law, Medicine, Education, Engineering and Business. It is the most international of Cambridge colleges with almost 70% of its students from overseas, and it is represented by alumni in 68 countries.

Miss Hughes developed an international network of students early in the College's life. As an advocate of co-education she would be delighted to see both men and women at Hughes Hall today: as early as 1894 she stated that, 'We shall never get first-rate training until men and women are trained together'. Hughes Hall's population has grown to over 600 students, and it has recently added significantly to the student accommodation on the periphery of the cricket field. Miss Hughes cared deeply about her students' welfare, and the college today upholds this philosophy. With a reputation for good food and hospitality, Hughes Hall is proud of the welcome it provides for its students.

ST EDMUND'S

When Henry Fitzalan Howard, 15th Duke of Norfolk, funded this college in 1896, he ended 224 years of exile from Cambridge University for Catholics, who had first been excluded from any public office by the Test Act of 1672. This was repealed nationally in 1828, but the University excluded non-Anglicans until 1871. The college's first leader was Father Edmond Nolan, former Vice-President of St Edmund's College, Ware. He came to Cambridge with four students on 23rd April, 1896, but the college's foundation date is kept as 2nd November, when they moved the present site.

Alongside its own members, St Edmunds provided lodging for graduates from other Cambridge colleges, many of whom wished to enter the priesthood. However, it was not long before most students came to the college already ordained, seeking a further teaching qualification. Student numbers increased just prior to WW1, and a new chapel was consecrated in 1916. The number of laymen at the college increased significantly in 1965, when the University included St Edmunds among four graduate colleges entitled to present their post-graduates for degrees.

In 1973 the Catholic Church generously signed away the college's present buildings and land to the Master and Fellows, and the college became an Approved Foundation in 1984. A six-storey tower was funded by the bequest of Honorary Fellow Dr Soichi Okinaga, President of Teiko University in Japan. It was opened on 30th April, 1993 by the Right Honourable Betty Boothroyd. The college today supports study and research in all academic areas, with a strong international element: two thirds of its members are from overseas, comprising over 50 different nationalities. St Edmunds began a new chapter in 2014 with the election of its new Master, the Hon. Matthew Bullock.

MURRAY EDWARDS

In 1954 Cambridge University had the lowest proportion of women undergraduates in the UK. New Hall was founded as the 3rd women's college since Girton and Newnham (Hughes Hall was not, at that time, officially a college of the University). In its first year, 16 students lodged in premises where Darwin College stands today. Members of the Darwin family gave their home, the Orchard, as the college site, where the first buildings were opened by Queen Elizabeth, the Queen Mother on the 5th of June 1965. The college was designed by Chamberlin, Powell and Bon, and its distinctive neo-Byzantine dome creates an elegant, inspiring space within. This underwent skillful renovation in the new millennium, when wiring and plumbing adaptations were concealed within the concrete.

Dame Rosemary Murray was appointed as the college's first President: a position she held for 28 years. Between 1975 and 1977 she also served as the first ever woman Vice-Chancellor in either Oxford or Cambridge University. In 2008 New Hall was re-named Murray Edwards College in her honour, along with a most generous benefactor: former alumna Ros Edwards who, with her husband Steve, donated £30 million.

The world-class college art collection acquires diverse and inspiring work by female artists and promotes the success of women early in their career. The library is a dramatic vaulted building whose elegant white arches continue the style and theme of the college's main dome. It holds 65,000 works, including an important selection of feminist literature.

The award-winning 'Transit of Venus' garden

Murray Edwards' exceptional gardens were planned and planted by Dame Rosemary Murray. Today's head gardener, Jo Cobb, has considered the students' diverse nationalities in her garden design, choosing an exciting variety of exotic plants as cheerful reminders of home for those far from their own country. There are also beautiful drifts of native British wild flowers. In 2007, the college became the first Cambridge college to enter a garden design in the Chelsea Flower Show. Sue Goss' design *Transit of Venus*, which celebrated the college's successes in astronomy, won a Bronze Flora medal.

Her design held a personal and historic significance, paying homage to her distant relative, the American mathematician William Harkness. In 1822 he had observed this rare movement of Venus across the sun. At that time he wrote:

> *'There will be no other till the twenty first century of our era has dawned upon the earth and the June flowers are blooming in 2004. What will be the state of science … God only knows.'*

122 years on college members, gardeners and all, gathered amongst the summer flowers to witness and fulfil his prediction.

In 2014 Murray Edwards celebrated its 60th anniversary. It aims to support young women during and beyond their time as students. Its alumna Dame Barbara Stocking, who was Chief Executive of Oxfam for 12 years, returned as College President in 2013. In her inaugural speech she stated.

> *'This College gave me the confidence and self-belief to make a contribution on the global stage and I am immensely grateful for that. I want to help today's talented young women play their part in shaping our future as tomorrow's thinkers and leaders'.*

CHURCHILL

I trust and believe that this College, this seed that we have sown, will grow to shelter and nurture generations who may add notably to the strength and happiness of our people, and to the knowledge and peaceful progress of the world. 'The mighty oak from an acorn towers; a tiny seed can fill a field with flowers'.

This was Sir Winston Churchill's vision: a college for the modern age that would promote collaboration between industry and universities. Building commenced on 17th October 1959, creating a national and Commonwealth memorial to Sir Winston which symbolises 'the gratitude of the English-speaking peoples' for his defence of freedom in the western world. The Churchill Archives Centre holds documents of many significant political figures including Sir Winston and three other British Prime Ministers. It is 'an invaluable resource for those working in British political, diplomatic, and military history of the 20th Century and beyond'. It also holds documents by eminent scientists since the Second World War.

Churchill specified that 70% of students should study mathematics or science. To support this, the college's first Master was nuclear physicist, Sir John Cockroft, followed by Sir William Hawthorne, a pioneer of the jet engine. Churchill has accrued more than 25 Nobel Prize winners to its name in just 60 years. Many are notable scientists, but there are also economists, and experts in the arts and humanities. The college, however, has never admitted a Theology student! Sir Winston's own Nobel Prize was for Literature. Modern art was a priority from the outset: an aluminium Gate sculpted by Geoffrey Clarke was commissioned when the college was first built. There are also busts of Churchill by Epstein and Nemon, and the college's art collection includes paintings by Sir Winston himself. In 1972 Churchill College became the first college to admit women students.

The college is set in a massive 40 acres of grounds, with an inspiring view of the city centre. The connecting courts contain a series of attractive gardens, and there are many imposing modern sculptures, including works by Barbara Hepworth. In 1992, the Møller Centre was opened. This elegant building, with its intriguing tower, is a major venue for conferences and management training.

Left: The distinctive tower of the Møller Centre
Right: 'Southern Shade' by Nigel Hall

DARWIN COLLEGE

The 1960s saw a serious national shortage of postgraduate places. Trinity, St John's and Gonville & Caius responded by jointly founding Darwin, Cambridge's first graduate-only college, in 1964. The oldest part of the college, Newnham Grange, was built in 1793 as the family home of a local coal and corn merchant. It was bought in 1885 by Sir George Darwin, who modified it, along with the adjacent Old Granary *(left)*. The property passed on to his son, Sir Charles, who died in 1962, and when it was put up for sale, the college's founders saw these buildings, with their superb position near the town centre and river, as ideal. Lady Darwin and her family supported the project enthusiastically and the name, Darwin College, was a natural choice for the new foundation.

In 1966 the college acquired the Hermitage, in Silver Street, and soon created the Rayne Building to link the two original houses. It progressively incorporated Newnham Terrace into the college and in 1994 built a new Study Centre to house a library and computer facilities. Darwin today provides a place of study and collaboration between Research Fellows, postdoctoral workers and students working towards Masters or Ph.D degrees in a wide range of subjects. It is one of the University's largest postgraduate colleges, with more than 630 students. The majority are from overseas, comprising over 50 nationalities.

LUCY CAVENDISH COLLEGE

Lucy Cavendish became a college for women graduates in 1965: the newest one for women in the United Kingdom. It is now the only Higher Education institution in Europe for women over 21. It owes its success to three Newnham alumni: Anna McClean Bidder, Kathleen Louise Wood-Legh, and Margaret Mary Braithwaite. They were experiencing frustration that women's access to fellowships within the University Colleges was limited to only Newnham or Girton, and resolved to increase opportunities for female graduates by creating a 'Third Foundation': a place for women to further their academic careers.

They had formed a Dining Group in 1950, which joined with another collective, led by Dame Myra Curtis, to persuade the University into founding New Hall in 1954. However, women with degrees could still not access the benefits of fellowship at the male colleges, and were isolated from this interactive stimulus. When the University sought to resolve matters, the Dining Group applied for recognition as the Lucy Cavendish Collegiate Society, which it gained in November 1964. It became an Approved Collegiate Society in 1965; its first resident student, Peggy Seay, came from America to study for a Ph.D in number theory. From its first offices in Silver Street it moved to two cottages along Northampton Street, before settling at Lady Margaret Road in 1970, with 10 graduate students. In 1972 it received its first 20 undergraduates: all mature students seeking 'to re-equip themselves for professional careers by advanced study, or by obtaining higher qualifications'. The college remains committed to helping women attain their full academic potential.

WOLFSON

Wolfson began in 1965 as University College, when the University itself perceived the needs of mature graduates coming from elsewhere to further their studies in Cambridge. It was initially based in Bredon House on the present site, when this was the only building, surrounded by orchard. The college gradually expanded, building accommodation, communal and conference facilities, and purchasing nearby properties. In 1973 the college name changed to Wolfson following a benefaction from the Wolfson Foundation; the resulting new buildings were opened in 1977 by Queen Elizabeth II.

The Lee Library was funded by a benefactor, Dr Lee Seng Tee, and was opened in 1994. It holds books supporting the masters and undergraduate courses at the college, and is especially designed for the convenience of advanced students writing major projects. Wolfson's academic community is diverse in its nationalities, and is renowned for its inclusive, informal working environment. Today the college comprises a wide variety of buildings interspersed with gardens. Its facilities provide excellent resources for high level studies, and also cater for visiting scholars' families.

Wolfson's exceptional grounds are given a sense of maturity by the trees retained from the gardens of the original houses, dating from the early 1900s. Other special features include a Judas Tree, a Tree Peony, and a wisteria-covered walk in Lee Court. There is an Oriental theme in the numerous sculptures, acknowledging the generosity of honorary Fellow, Mr S.T. Lee, who funded Wolfson's excellent library.

CLARE HALL

Clare Hall positively supports family life. Its first buildings, designed by Ralph Erskine, included 20 apartments, 7 of which were created for families. The college also arranges special children's activities, swimming lessons and monthly family meals.

Clare Hall was also part of the 1960s initiative to provide more fellowship posts in the University, at a time when both research and diversity of graduate teaching were developing rapidly. Clare College was keen to create post-graduate provision, but opinions varied on what form this should take: might a separate centre be provided, or could more senior academics be brought into the existing College fellowship? The dilemma of Clare's Governing Body was resolved by Richard Eden, who suggested that

> *'the aim should be to establish a Society of Fellows primarily engaged in advanced study, to bring together an international community of scholars and Cambridge University lecturers and professors'.*

The first Master, Brian Pippard, was elected in 1965, and Clare Hall opened in 1966. Clare College provided its first land and buildings, and remained its trustee until 1984, when it became an independent college within the University. The college's visiting fellow programme has greatly raised Clare Hall's academic profile, which attracts scholars from all continents and specialisms, and its alumni include two Nobel Prize winners. In 2000 it hosted the prestigious Tanner Symposium: a series of lectures marking the millennium, and also hosts the annual Cambridge Tanner Lectures.

The sculpture 'Triangulum', by John Sydney Carter, was designed to mark Clare Hall's 50th Anniversary

Sir Denys Lasdun's innovative modern design

The Grove

FITZWILLIAM

For nearly a century, Fitzwilliam House was opposite the museum with which it shares its name, providing access to a Cambridge education for less affluent students. In 1963 it moved to Huntingdon Road, and became Fitzwilliam College in 1966, when the college's new buildings, by Sir Denys Lasdun, were finished. These form a striking contrast to the original house, *The Grove*, which had formerly belonged to the Darwin family. Building has continued in adventurous architectural style, culminating with the Olisa Library, opened in 2010.

Fitzwilliam's varied and distinctive buildings are linked by skilfully planted gardens which soften the bold contours of the architecture. It is proud to utilise modern energy-saving measures in its newest buildings, and in 2012 was ranked fourth in the inter-college Green League. The college became co-educational in 1978, and today is home to 450 undergraduates, 300 graduates and 60 fellows. True to its origins, it combines Cambridge college traditions with an unpretentious, inclusive atmosphere where ability, not background, matters most.

HOMERTON

Homerton's origins go back to London in 1730, when the Congregational church founded a society to train young men as ministers. It convened every week at an inn, and became known as the 'King's Head Society'. In 1768 it bought premises of its own in Homerton High Street for 12 students and their tutor. In 1850 this became a specialist teacher training college for both men and women destined for schools run by the Congregational Board of Education.

In 1894 Homerton moved from the industrialised East End to today's buildings in Hills Road, Cambridge, which were vacated by the defunct Cavendish College. At this time, a mixed college was quite unacceptable to Cambridge University, so Homerton changed to admit women only. However, it reverted to being co-educational on becoming an Approved Society in 1976. By 2000 Homerton had expanded considerably, and in 2001 began to offer the University's full academic range of courses, of which teaching degrees have now become a small element. In 2010, Homerton received its Royal Charter as a full College. Homerton's spacious grounds and buildings offer its students the rare luxury of accommodation throughout their course.

The library includes a unique collection of 9,000 children's books, and in the Victorian Great Hall, students occasionally enjoy 'Harry Potter Formal Halls', complete with real owls flying overhead! Students rate it one of the friendliest colleges in Cambridge, despite the fact that it is the largest: Trinity is the only other college with over 1000 students.

Right: The Cavendish Building
Left: The Great Hall

Bridge over Bin Brook

ROBINSON

The modern exterior of Robinson College gives no clue to the vast, verdant space within, which comprises ten original Edwardian gardens. At the heart of the grounds is a wild woodland area and a lake, which is fed by a stream called Bin Brook. It is a secluded haven for students, visitors and wildlife alike. A patient observer on the walkway by the brook may spot a water vole; deer are sometimes seen. The college is part of the National Gardens Scheme, and its carpets of Spring bulbs can rival the displays at Sidney Sussex and Christ's.

Robinson College is the newest college in the University. It admitted its first undergraduates in 1979 thanks to Sir David Robinson's donation of £18 million, and was opened by Queen Elizabeth II in 1981. The college layout, designed by Gillespie, Kidd and Coia, forms a 'double ribbon' of buildings on the perimeter of the site. There are elements of a castle theme evoked in the drawbridge-like sloping path up to the large gate and tower at the entrance. The buildings are faced with one and a quarter million handmade bricks, and the façade is softened by a 'portcullis' style trellis.

Sir David was a remarkable philanthropist and entrepreneur. His fortune came chiefly from his television and rentals business and, later, horse racing. The Robinson Charitable Trust donated funds for Addenbrookes Hospital's Rosie Maternity Unit, named after his mother, and also the Evelyn Nursing Home and Papworth Hospital. After the Penlee lifeboat tragedy in 1981, he paid £400,000 for a new lifeboat, and later provided the RNLI with three more. Sir David died in 1987, six years after the death of his son.

Robinson is the only Cambridge college to have been founded as co-educational from the outset. In keeping with its modern, inclusive values, the chapel was created by a partnership of denominations; there are only two University places of worship with this distinction. It features some striking artwork. The main door, and gate linking the side and main chapels, feature beautiful bronze work by I. Metzstein, depicting the waters of baptism and the vine of life.

The chapel's stained glass is exceptional, created by artist John Piper, who also designed the windows for Coventry cathedral after WW2. Sir David especially asked him to create imagery that would appeal to religious and non-religious alike, and the rich colours of the abstract *Light of the World* window are truly uplifting. The chapel also has a remarkable modern organ: one of only three in England designed by Erik Frobenius.

Above: The Chapel's impressive stained glass
Right: Robinson's castle-inspired architecture

Wesley House

Westminster College

CAMBRIDGE THEOLOGICAL FEDERATION

'Roots down, Walls down, Bridges out'

This is the ethos of the Cambridge Theological Federation, formed in 1972. Today, nine member institutes are involved in the education of Christian leaders, and in the study of relations between Christians, Jews and Muslims. The four earliest members featured here resource people for ministry and service in the Christian Church.

WESLEY HOUSE

This is a cross-cultural community of scholars and students in the Wesleyan tradition. Founded in 1921 to give access for British Methodist ministers to a Cambridge education whilst living in a community of prayer and spiritual formation, today it welcomes lay and ordained people from all over the world to study on formal degree programmes, sabbaticals and short courses. During 2015 the buildings were substantially remodelled to provide updated accommodation. The new gatehouse fronting onto Jesus Lane contains a library, archive, teaching rooms and a roof top refectory. The college hopes that its graduates will exert a thoughtful and transformative influence in their communities, as theological educators, visionary church leaders, or by developing theological responses to the problems facing our world.

WESTMINSTER COLLEGE

'Imagine a beautiful place, a welcoming community, a place and people ready for prayer and learning and life. Imagine Westminster!'

Westminster College began in 1844 as the college of the Presbyterian Church in England, giving lectures at Exeter Hall in London, and later Queen's Square. It moved to Cambridge in 1899 when twin sisters Agnes Smith Lewis and Margaret Dunlop Gibson gave the college's site to the Church. They taught themselves many ancient languages, including biblical ones, and travelled through Europe and the Middle East, including visits to St Catherine's monastery at Mount Sinai. They received honorary doctorates for their significant contributions to biblical scholarship. Westminster merged with Cheshunt College in 1967. A recently created prayer labyrinth in the grounds symbolises the college's wish to be not only a forum for dynamic debate, but offer a place of rest and contemplation, to achieve clarity in a chaotic world.

Westcott House

Ridley Hall

WESTCOTT HOUSE

This Anglican college has 75 students, preparing for ministry. Brooke Foss Westcott set up the Cambridge Clergy Training School in 1881, which was renamed for him after his death in 1901. He believed that the Church of England's inter-doctrinal conflicts were a counterproductive diversion from the true spirit of the scripture, saying, 'I only wish men would pay more attention to acting and less to dogmatising'. He endeavoured to reflect the selfless example of Christ's life in his own, and inspired many passive, affluent churchgoers into actively assisting the poor and unemployed. His defence of miners in the strike of 1892 exemplified this, for his actions lost him appointment as Archbishop of York. The college continues to work in the spirit he established, with students from a wide range of backgrounds forming a 'community of differences', rooted in a life of daily prayer, theological study and public ministry.

RIDLEY HALL

In 1881 Ridley Hall welcomed its first eight students to train as ordained ministers. Today around 140 men and women study, pray and live together in this beautiful college at any one time and it has established identity as a vibrant evangelical Anglican college. A range of courses provides students with a recognised qualification while preparing them for ministry, whether as children's workers, parish priests or theological educators. The college offers a distinctive ethos, seeking to respond faithfully and imaginatively to the changing dynamics of Church and society.

'We are passionate for men and women to be convinced
of the love of God, live lives of service,
and articulate the Gospel - with clarity, power and hope -
to our rapidly changing world'

5
mph
8
kmh

Blaze of Glory? Victorious crews wear a leafy emblem of their success

ROWING

From a distance, the slender boats appear to glide with a grace that suggests effortless elegance. Only close up can one appreciate the awesome surges of power produced by eight determined rowers. The Cam is a seed bed for oarsmen who may go on to be selected for the mighty crew that competes in the world renowned Oxford-Cambridge Boat Race. This annual contest has taken place on the Thames in London since 1829. Cambridge rowers reserve several unprintable terms for their arch-rivals at Oxford, but can currently smile at their overall superiority. In the Boat Race they boast 82 wins against Oxford's 79, and hold the record number of consecutive victories, between 1924 and 1936. They also established the current course record in 1998 when they recorded an average speed of 15.5 miles per hour.

But there is much more to Cambridge rowing than this. For many, rowing is an all-consuming passion, often with training sessions at least once each day. Because the Cam is too narrow for side-by-side competition bumping was devised in 1827, and has grown into an unshakeable Cambridge tradition. Over 170 college crews participate in 'the Bumps' known as *Lents*, which take place in February during the Lent term, and *Mays*, held during the Easter term. Crews are organised into four divisions, using the previous year's finishing order as the new season's starting point. A cannon gives the starting signal, and boats set off from Baits Bite Lock at one-and-a-half length intervals, aiming to literally bump the boat in front. This is a frenetic process, fuelled by vociferous bankside support. Many years ago a rower was killed by the sharp prow of a boat which overran while bumping. Boats now have a protective knob affixed to prevent injury, but coxswains are required to acknowledge bumps immediately by raising a hand, and both boats pull over as the rest sweep past. Successful crews wear a leafy branch to advertise their victory. Larger colleges muster more crews, but vigorous support, and iron resolve can overcome the toughest odds. Sidney Sussex, with only ten men, once managed to come seventh overall. Heroic verse celebrates their victory:

'There were eight to row and one to steer,
And one to run on the banks and cheer.'

Over four days' competition, boats move up the starting order according to success. Champions are crowned Head of the River. They and any crew which goes up four or more, win their oars: literally full-size wooden oars painted in college livery and listing the crew and their defeated boats. The victorious crew traditionally celebrates with the ritual burning of a boat.

Rowing has evolved its own intriguing vocabulary. An experienced boatie uses an oar known as a cleaver. A novice will need to learn how to use his spoon (the painted part of the oar) taking care to feather it in a horizontal position as it travels over the water, before squaring to enter perpendicular to catch the next stroke. Failure may result in catching a crab: dipping too deep and at an angle (in extreme cases ejecting the oarsman from the boat). Frequent crabbing may earn the rower a reputation as a kipper. No-one wishes to be known as a quiche ('real men don't eat quiche') which implies ineffectual or lazy performance. But it is just as bad to be a spanner who allows panic to override good technique at the expense of speed. Bumping may be averted by washing off a fast-approaching boat with a wave thrown up by the rudder, and a speedy eight may achieve an overbump, by catching the crew that started three boats ahead. Meanwhile, among the spectators, buftys will reminisce about their own glorious rowing days.

Previous Page: The Lent Bumps
Overleaf: New Court, St John's College

PUNTING

The River Cam has been the town's life-blood for over 2,000 years. Cambridge grew rich because of its trading potential. Until the 1600s the centre could be accessed from the sea, and light vessels continued to use the river for trade until the railway came in 1845. Declining industrial use of the river, combined with new town drainage systems improved its water quality. As pollution abated, the river became popular for recreation. College rowing, made famous by the annual Oxford vs Cambridge Boat Race, takes place downstream from the town. Meanwhile, along the college Backs and upstream in the water meadows, the leisurely punt rules. These flat-bottomed boats were designed for the transportation of goods and livestock, but now provide unique vantage points to admire the beauty of Cambridge.

Endless amusement may be derived from observing activity along the river, where 'Chauffeur punts' cruise expertly between the novices zig-zagging randomly from bank to bank. If you wish to try punting for yourself, stand bravely on the platform at the back of the punt. It is easiest to steer if you hold the pole behind, rather than at the side; you can use it as a rudder by trailing it in the water at the appropriate angle. A passenger can use the paddle to help avoid inconvenient walls, bridges, or other punts. Lean on the pole to propel the punt, twisting it slightly to release it from the mud: a vital precaution, as the tales of stranded punters are no myth. Strong ankles and flexible knees are an advantage. Head for the highest part of any bridge, and remain calm in the face of willow branches. In the event of collision, smile sweetly.

The nature of your Cambridge punting experience depends very much on choice of time and place. Chauffeur punters are ever-present around Quayside and Silver Street, and will provide commentary on your journey, though their historical accuracy may be questionable. Naturalists will be enchanted by the early morning trip from Silver Street to Grantchester, when bird life can be seen and heard in abundance, and the soft light creates enchanting ripples and reflections. Until recently, this was a traditional trip for May Ball 'survivors', punting to Grantchester at dawn for early breakfast at the Orchard Tea Garden. Historians may prefer the Backs. This is the stretch between Quayside and Silver Street where the colleges' tranquillity seems preserved from centuries ago, particularly in the early morning or late evening.

Either trip will appeal to the romantic, but a candlelit journey might be the most special of all, particularly if accompanied by a cosy rug and bottle of wine. By contrast, the fun of joining the throng with a group of friends on a sunny afternoon, getting tangled in the willow branches and drifting helplessly sideways into the course of a 'bus punt' full of tourists, could become the happiest of Cambridge memories.

Right: King's Bridge
Opposite: Garret Hostel Bridge
Overleaf: Clare Bridge

The Bridge of Sighs, St John's

THE BOTANIC GARDEN

Cambridge Botanic Garden, founded in 1762 'for the benefit of mankind', first occupied a five acre site donated by Trinity's Rev. R. Walker. Set between Downing Street and Free School Lane, that garden emulated the Physic Garden at Chelsea. Charles Darwin's teacher, Steven Henslow believed that the study of plants had more to offer than just their medicinal properties and proposed the move to a larger site. Land was acquired from Trinity Hall in 1831 and the new garden opened 15 years later, on November 2nd 1846. The first curator, Andrew Murray, devised the basic layout with its winding path around the circumference, the lake, magnificent arboretum and systematic beds. The gates from the original garden were relocated to the Trumpington Road side by Hobson's conduit, from which the new garden takes its water supply. Today's entrance is via award-winning new gates on the corner of Brookside and Trumpington Road.

The Garden is a research centre of international significance, containing around 8,000 plant species. The Glasshouse Range displays 2,000 specimens in carefully replicated jungle, desert and alpine environments. With a focus on aspects of climate change, ecology and sustainable horticulture, there is a policy of minimal irrigation and chemical intervention. A weather station supplying data to the Meteorological Office at Bracknell is also located here. The Garden's newest development, the Sainsbury Laboratory, houses the University Herbarium: a collection of over 1,000,000 pressed plant specimens, including some collected by Charles Darwin. Photographic images taken by Darwin during his voyage on the Beagle have been etched into metal plates and displayed outside the recently opened café.

The Garden's main purpose may be scientific study, but its beauty enchants visitors of all ages. In addition to the world famous glasshouses, there are rose and lavender collections, fenland and chalkland areas, and a newly created wildflower meadow. Children love to run in the grass maze and explore the rockery. The fountain, designed by silversmith David Mellor, fascinates everybody. Even in the depths of winter there are areas filled with colour, scent and a wonderful tapestry of natural forms. Wildlife is abundant: many bird species are attracted by the diverse trees. Ducks and moorhens frequent the lake, where there are also many fish. Whether you choose to wander through the grounds, or find a shady sanctuary to absorb the peace, the Botanic Garden is a perennial joy.

The Mill Pool

GRANTCHESTER

Grantchester, a quintessentially rural English village just upstream of the city, is a separate place and yet an essential part of the Cambridge experience. This small settlement, with twisty roads and thatched cottages is worlds away from the grandeur of the colleges. Even in the heat of a busy Summer afternoon there is a pervading peace, as if the wattle and daub walls of the old cottages absorb noise. The traditional way to visit is by punt or via a footpath, known as the Grantchester Grind, which winds from Newnham, alongside the river through the water meadows. Either way, your journey may work up a thirst and a healthy appetite. Fortunately there are several pubs in the village to revive you, not to mention the historic Orchard Tea Garden.

Here at the Orchard, a green pavilion set amidst the apple trees remains much as it was at the turn of the century, when poet Rupert Brooke and his friends, Bertrand Russell, E.M. Forster and Virginia Woolf came here to escape the demands of academic life. A small museum, dedicated to Brooke, is now adjacent to the tearoom. In spring, while relaxing in a deck chair beneath the apple blossom and listening to birdsong, time seems to stand still: this is a wonderful place to reclaim the peace of a bygone era. Today's Cambridge students still seek refreshment here, although in recent years the charming tradition of punting upriver at dawn, for an early champagne breakfast after the May Balls, has become a thing of the past.

The Green Man

Grantchester has always attracted poets. Tennyson and Chaucer both refer to the mill, which burnt down in 1928, and Byron is said to have loved swimming a little further upstream in the secluded pool, which is still named after him. William Wordsworth, in his autobiographical poem *The Prelude*, recalls the peace he enjoyed where,

'Beside the pleasant Mill of Trompington
I laughed with Chaucer in the hawthorn shade'.

In the centre of the village, St Mary's church proudly displays its connections with Corpus Christi College through its pelican and lily insignia. St Mary's has been a central focus in the recent television drama series, *Grantchester*. However, it is Rupert Brooke who originally secured Grantchester's fame. The village is immortalised in his poem, *The Old Vicarage, Grantchester*, where the young man had lodgings for a while. At that time, the church clock was not working. In later years, while staying in the Café de Westens, far away in Berlin, Brooke yearned for the timeless tranquillity of his former sanctuary, symbolised by the clock's unmoving hands:

'...And laughs the immortal river still
Under the mill, under the mill?
Say, is there Beauty yet to find?
And Certainty? and Quiet kind?
Deep meadows yet, for to forget
The lies, the truths, and pain?... oh! yet
Stands the church clock at ten to three?
And is there honey still for tea?'

St Mary's Church

In the 1950s, two more poets discovered the pleasures of wandering in the fields around Grantchester. Ted Hughes and his future wife, Sylvia Plath, spent many hours here absorbing the tranquillity together: a fleeting calm before the storms which later blighted their relationship. Sylvia wrote in a letter to her mother,

> *'Got up at 4.30 am this day with Ted and went for a long walk to Grantchester … I felt a peace and joy in the most beautiful world with animals and birds … we began mooing at a pasture of cows, and they all looked up, and as if hypnotised, began to follow us in a crowd of about twenty across the pasture to a wooden stile, staring fascinated. I stood on the stile, and in a resonant voice, recited all I knew of Chaucer's Canterbury Tales for about twenty minutes. I never had such an intelligent, fascinated audience'.*

Above: Grantchester Meadows
Left: The Orchard Tea Rooms

THE AMERICAN CEMETERY, MADINGLEY

Nothing can prepare the visitor for the emotional impact of this vast, elegant memorial, which was created on land donated by Cambridge University, and dedicated on July 16th, 1956. The immaculate perfection of its tranquil setting on Madingley Hill is starkly poignant in the light of its brutal and tragic history. This is the only American World War II cemetery in the British Isles, graced with 3,812 pure white marble headstones: 3,732 Latin crosses, and 80 Stars of David for Jewish servicemen. These are arranged in arcs, radiating from a central pole where the American flag flies – the final resting places for members of the American armed forces, who gave their lives in World War II. The Wall of the Missing, an immense screen 427 feet long, is reflected in three narrow oblong pools which run along its full length. Close inspection will bring the chilling discovery that this entire wall is filled with the names of 5,127 more members of the American forces lost between 1942 and 1945, who 'rest in unknown graves'.

The chapel stands at the far end of the Wall. Inside, there is an immense campaign map on one side, engraved by David Kindersley's Cambridge workshop, and dramatic illustrations of aircraft on the blue painted 'sky' of the ceiling. A bronze inscription over the east doorway to the chapel reads, 'Into thy hands, o Lord', and on the north side there is a further inscription in the stone: 'Grant unto them o Lord eternal rest'. There is also a Visitor Centre and exhibition, where staff are available to provide more detailed information on those commemorated here.

Statues representing the different elements of the United States armed forces keep a silent vigil along the Wall of the Missing. Airman, soldier, Coast Guardsman and sailor watch protectively over the headstones: a memory of Americans set amongst the peaceful English landscape that they helped to defend.

ACKNOWLEDGEMENTS

Our sincere thanks go to the Masters, Bursars, Archivists, and Fellows of all the colleges, along with the creators of their respective websites. We are indebted to Dr Keith Carne, Jennifer Brook, Timothy Harvey-Samuel, Christopher Lawrence, Richard Berg-Rust, Dr Roger Lovatt, Professor Geoffrey Thorndike Martin, Nicholas Rogers, Matthew Moss, Dr Martin Brett, Jenny Ulph, Elizabeth Ennion-Smith, Carol Lamb, Dr Lucy Hughes, Dr Ronald Hyam, Dr Elisabeth Leedham-Green, Syd Harper, Rev'd Martin Seeley, Jane Leach, Jonathan Holmes, Caroline Sier, Dr Frances Wilmoth, Mr Grainger, Jonathan Smith, Dr John Pollard, Fiona Duffy, Elizabeth Stratton, Jayne Ringrose, Amanda Goode, Jo Tynan, Alexandra Browne, David Ibbetson, Dona McCullagh. In addition we thank the many secretaries and porters who kindly helped along our enquiries. We are also grateful to the Trinity First and Third Rowing Club website. We are also indebted to John Willis Clark M.A, F.S.A, of Trinity College, whose thorough historical work has been indispensable.

Special thanks to Sheila for her expert editing. Loving gratitude to Juliette for her assistance with design and editing, cheerful encouragement, and kind provision of timely refreshments. Our 'canine therapists' Dyson and Izzy, have comforted and refreshed us when the burden seemed most heavy.

Above: Irises at Christ's College
Right: Autumn crocus at Queens' College

BIBLIOGRAPHY

A Concise Guide to the Town and University of Cambridge, J.W. Clark (Macmillan & Bowes 1902) ***Cambridge: Historical and Picturesque Notes,*** J.W. Clark (Seeley & Co. Ltd. 1890) ***Cambridge Colleges,*** J. Jeacock (Jarrold Publishing 2003) ***Portrait of Cambridge,*** C. R. Benstead (Robert Hayle 1968) ***Cambridge,*** J. Steegman (B.T. Batsford Ltd 1945) ***The University of Cambridge: an 800th Anniversary Portrait,*** Editor: P. Pagnamenta (Third Millennium Publishing 2008) ***In Praise of Cambridge,*** S. Waterlow (Constable & Co. Ltd 1912) ***The Story of Cambridge*** S Boyd (Cambridge University Press 2005) ***Cambridge,*** M. Hall (Pevensey 2000) ***Live the City: Cambridge,*** M. White (Live the City Publishing 2009) ***King's College Chapel,*** J. Warrior (Tim Rawle Associates 2001) ***Cambridge Gardens,*** Gray & Frankl (Pevensey Press 1984) ***Cambridge,*** N. Barwell (Blackie & Son) ***The Night Climbers of Cambridge,*** Whipplesnaith (Chatto & Windus 1937) ***Cambridge Street Names,*** Gray & Stubbings (Cambridge University Press 2000) ***Cambridge & its Colleges,*** A. Hamilton Thompson (Methuen & Co. 1910) ***Francis Frith's Around Cambridge,*** C. Tully (Frith Book Co. Ltd. 1999) ***Leaflets of Local Lore,*** Urbs Camboritum (Newton & Denney 1976) ***Cambridge American Cemetery & Memorial,*** American Battle Monuments Commission ***Devas & Pearce's Cambridge,*** C. Devas (Midsummer Publishing 2001) ***Cambridge: A Photographic Celebration,*** K. Wallis (Fotogenix Publishing 2004) ***A Cambridge Keepsake,*** D. Pearce (Fotogenix Publishing 2005)

ABOUT THIS BOOK

During the last 20 years, Andrew Pearce's photographs have extensively documented the changing nature of Cambridge. The city has evolved steadily throughout history but, as one of Britain's key centres of scientific and commercial growth, it is now developing at an unprecedented rate. The Science Parks, Cambridge's vast biomedical campus at Addenbrookes, and the new University North-West site are providing many employment opportunities, and Cambridge's proximity to London makes it a natural choice for building new homes.

What will be the cost? Cambridge's ancient city centre is becoming an island of tradition and history in a sea of new development that has rendered the area unrecognisable in places. And that precious tranquillity, praised by so many wise and thoughtful people, is under threat from the ever-increasing levels of traffic noise that permeate the atmosphere at all but the earliest hours of the day. Of all places, Cambridge should be able to make wise and well-informed decisions; to act as responsible custodians of this national treasure. Will we be able to strike a balance between development of land and degradation of environment, modernism and brutalism in architecture, profit for the present and prosperity for the future?

This book aims to capture the precious subtleties that make Cambridge unique: the mellow ancient stonework, the inspired new buildings, the beautiful college gardens and, especially, the remarkable balance that exists between the town and the natural world. Cambridge's charm lies in its intimacy, and the small details of life in its narrow streets and peaceful river. As the city rushes headlong into the future, these are the things this book hopes to celebrate: it is dedicated to all those who work to nurture and preserve the beauty of this very special place.

Andrew Pearce, April 2018

Right: Excellence in modern architecture is exemplified at Wolfson College

INDEX

Previous page: King's College from the Pitt Building
Left & opposite: Ornament detail, Christ's College

INDEX

A PARTING VIEW OF CAMBRIDGE

And yet the spectacle may well demand
A more substantial name, no mimic show,
Itself a living part of a live whole,
A creek in a vast sea; for, all degrees
And shapes of spurious fame and short-lived praise
Here sate in state, and fed with daily alms
Retainers won away from solid good.
And here was Labour; his own bond-slave; Hope
That never set the pains against the prize;
Idleness halting with his weary clog,
And poor misguided Shame, and witless Fear,
And simple Pleasure foraging for Death;
Honour misplaced, and Dignity astray;
Feuds, factions, flatteries, enmity and guile
Murmuring submission, and bald government,
(The idol weak as the idolator),
And Decency and Custom starving Truth,
And blind Authority beating with his staff
The child that might have led him; Emptiness
Followed as of good omen, and meek Worth
Left to herself unheard of and unknown.

William Wordsworth, 1770-1850

the concluding lines of *The Prelude*:
Wordsworth's poem about his life at Cambridge

Right: Aconites by King's Chapel
Overleaf: St John's Bridge of Sighs